Selected Poems

JOHN DRYDEN

DOVER · THRIFT · EDITIONS

Selected Poems

JOHN DRYDEN

DOVER PUBLICATIONS, INC.
Mineola, New York

DOVER THRIFT EDITIONS

GENERAL EDITOR: PAUL NEGRI
EDITOR OF THIS VOLUME: JOSLYN T. PINE

Published in the United Kingdom by David & Charles, Brunel House, Forde Close, Newton Abbot, Devon, TQ12 4PU.

Bibliographical Note

This Dover edition, first published in 2002, is a new selection of John Dryden's poetry from the Cambridge Edition of *The Poetical Works of John Dryden* edited by George R. Noyes, published in 1908 by Houghton Mifflin Company, Boston and New York. The Introduction is Part I of the "Biographical Sketch" by Mr. Noyes from the same work. His prefatory notes and footnotes, which are included selectively and in some instances slightly abridged, are also from the Cambridge Edition. All bracketed footnotes were specially prepared for the Dover edition. All the poems contained herein are unabridged.

Library of Congress Cataloging-in-Publication Data

Dryden, John, 1631–1700.
   [Poems. Selections]
   Selected poems / John Dryden.
      p. cm. — (Dover thrift editions)
   Includes bibliographical references and indexes.
   ISBN 0-486-42047-7 (pbk.)
    I. Title. II. Series.

PR3412 2002
821".4—dc21

                                    2002017466

Manufactured in the United States of America
Dover Publications, Inc., 31 East 2nd Street, Mineola, N.Y. 11501

Introduction

JOHN DRYDEN [1631–1700] is the greatest and the most representative English man of letters of the last quarter of the seventeenth century. From the death of Milton in 1674 to his own in 1700 no other writer can compare with him in versatility and power; indeed, in the varied character of his work, as dramatist, satirist, controversialist, translator, and critic, he has few rivals in the entire history of English literature. Though he composed his most important original poems to serve some passing political purpose, he made them immortal by his literary genius. Half unconsciously he became the founder of a literary school that retained its preeminence for more than a hundred years after his death. Any account of his life should deal primarily with his writings and with the political events that gave the occasion for many of them; at the same time it should pay due heed to Dryden's own personality, which has not always been treated with the respect that it deserves. Dryden was by profession a writer, not a hero or prophet; he suffers by the inevitable comparison with his great contemporary Milton. Yet, beneath his superficial inconsistency he had a large general honesty and uprightness, and the fierce invective of his satires must not blind us to his kindliness and generosity. Though not heroic, Dryden is eminently lovable.

Dryden's parents were landed gentry. His father, Erasmus Dryden, third son of Sir Erasmus Dryden, baronet, married on October 21, 1630, Mary, daughter of the Reverend Henry Pickering, rector of Aldwincle All Saints, in Northamptonshire. John Dryden, the first of the fourteen children of this marriage, is said to have been born on August 9, 1631,[1] at the parsonage house of Aldwincle All Saints, the residence of his mother's parents. He was brought up under strongly Puritan influences, since both the Drydens and the Pickerings took the side of the Parliament in its conflict against Charles I. He was educated

---

[1][T]his date rests on no better authority than a note by Pope, first printed in the 1735 edition of his works.

first at Westminster School in London, under the famous master, Dr. Busby, to whom he later sent his own sons; and next at Trinity College, Cambridge, where he matriculated in July, 1650, and where he took his bachelor's degree in January, 1654.

The Conclusion Book of Trinity College records that in July, 1652, Dryden was disciplined for "his disobedience to the vice master, and his contumacy in taking his punishment inflicted by him." A pleasanter glimpse of the young poet is given in a letter quoted by Mr. Christie:[2] "Dryden . . . was reckoned a man of good parts and learning while in college: he had . . . read over and very well understood all the Greek and Latin poets. He stayed to take his bachelor's degree, but his head was too roving and active, or what else you'll call it, to confine himself to a college life; and so he left it and went to London into gayer company, and set up for a poet, which he was as well qualified for as any man."[3]

While at school and college Dryden had made some trifling experiments in writing verse. At Westminster School he had translated, as "a Thursday-night's exercise," the *Third Satire of Persius*, and had composed in honor of his deceased schoolmate, Lord Hastings, an elegy which is still preserved. In 1650 he prefixed a short complimentary poem to *Sion and Parnassus*, a collection of religious poems by his friend John Hoddesdon. In 1655 he wrote a curious letter to his cousin Honor Driden, mingling verse and prose in a strain of conventional and not too delicate gallantry. These early pieces are full of extravagant conceits of the school of Cowley[4], and show at the best only a boyish dexterity in copying a prevailing literary fashion.

Nothing is known of Dryden's life between 1654 and 1658. In June, 1654, his father had died, leaving to him, as the eldest son, landed property which yielded about forty pounds a year, enough at that time to support a single man in decent comfort. A year later, if the heading of the letter to Honor Driden be correct, he was still at Cambridge. From this fantastic epistle, which indicates nothing more than a college flirtation, some critics have strangely concluded that the young poet was seriously in love with his cousin. Whether he continued to reside in Cambridge, or returned to his father's estate after 1655, cannot positively be determined. If Shadwell[5] is correct in speaking of him, "when he came first to town," as "a raw young fellow of seven and

---

[2][W. D. Christie is a noted nineteenth-century Dryden scholar. —ED.]
[3][From] *Select Poems by Dryden*, ed. Christie and Firth, Oxford, 1893, page xvi.
[4][Abraham Cowley (1618–1667) was one of the English metaphysical poets. —ED.]
[5][Thomas Shadwell (c. 1642–1692) was an English dramatist and poet who succeeded Dryden as poet laureate. —ED.]

twenty," he did not remove to London and "set up for a poet" until 1658.

Dryden's life after his settlement in London may be conveniently divided into three periods: the first ending in 1681, the second in 1688, and the third with his death in 1700. In the first period, after a few occasional poems, Dryden chose the drama as the most profitable field of literary work, and by his success in it became the leading English man of letters of his time. In 1681, having from a number of causes become thoroughly dissatisfied with his occupation as a playwright, he turned to satire and controversial writing, both in prose and verse, and brought his consummate literary skill to the service of the royal power and the Tory party. By the Revolution of 1688, he was deprived of his position as a court favorite, and thrown back upon his pen for support. After some attempts, only partially successful, to recover his position as a popular dramatist, he found a congenial occupation as a translator of the Greek and Latin poets, and as a modernizer of Chaucer.

Contents

Selected Poems

JOHN DRYDEN

ANNUS MIRABILIS*

THE YEAR OF WONDERS, 1666

An historical poem containing the progress and various successes of our naval war with Holland, under the conduct of His Highness Prince Rupert, and His Grace the Duke of Albemarle; and describing the Fire of London.

Multum interest res poscat, an homines latius imperare velint.
TRAJAN IMPERATOR *ad Plin.*

Urbs antiqua ruit, multos dominata per annos. —VIRG.

[*Annus Mirabilis* was licensed for the press on November 22, 1666, and was published in a tiny octavo, date 1667. . . . The present edition follows the text of 1688, which was apparently slightly revised by Dryden.]

I

In thriving arts long time had Holland grown,
    Crouching at home and cruel when abroad;
Scarce leaving us the means to claim our own;
    Our king they courted, and our merchants aw'd.

II

Trade, which like blood should circularly flow,
    Stopp'd in their channels, found its freedom lost:
Thither the wealth of all the world did go,
    And seem'd but ship-wrack'd on so base a coast.

---

*[The lettered footnotes in this poem are Dryden's. —ED.]

III

For them alone the heav'ns had kindly heat;
  In eastern quarries ripening precious dew:[a]
For them the Idumæan balm did sweat,
  And in hot Ceylon spicy forests grew.

IV

The sun but seem'd the lab'rer of their year;
  Each waxing moon supplied her wat'ry store,[b]
To swell those tides, which from the line did bear
  Their brim-full vessels to the Belgian shore.

V

Thus mighty in her ships stood Carthage long,
  And swept the riches of the world from far;
Yet stoop'd to Rome, less wealthy, but more strong;
  And this may prove our second Punic war.

VI

What peace can be, where both to one pretend?
  (But they more diligent, and we more strong)
Or if a peace, it soon must have an end;
  For they would grow too pow'rful were it long.

VII

Behold two nations then, ingag'd so far,
  That each sev'n years the fit must shake each land:
Where France will side to weaken us by war,
  Who only can his vast designs withstand.

VIII

See how he feeds th' Iberian[c] with delays,
  To render us his timely friendship vain:
And while his secret soul on Flanders preys,
  He rocks the cradle of the babe of Spain.

---

[a]*In eastern quarries*, &c. Precious stones at first are dew, condens'd and harden'd by the warmth of the sun or subterranean fires.
[b]*Each waxing*, &c. According to their opinion, who think that great heap of waters under the line is depress'd into tides by the moon, towards the poles.
[c]*Th' Iberian*. The Spaniard.

IX

Such deep designs of empire does he lay
   O'er them whose cause he seems to take in hand;
And, prudently, would make them lords at sea,
   To whom with ease he can give laws by land.

X

This saw our king; and long within his breast
   His pensive counsels balanc'd to and fro:
He griev'd the land he freed should be oppress'd,
   And he less for it than usurpers do.

XI

His gen'rous mind the fair ideas drew
   Of fame and honor, which in dangers lay;
Where wealth, like fruit on precipices, grew,
   Not to be gather'd but by birds of prey.

XII

The loss and gain each fatally were great;
   And still his subjects call'd aloud for war;
But peaceful kings, o'er martial people set,
   Each other's poise and counterbalance are.

XIII

He, first, survey'd the charge with careful eyes,
   Which none but mighty monarchs could maintain;
Yet judg'd, like vapors that from limbecs rise,
   It would in richer showers descend again.

XIV

At length resolv'd t' assert the wat'ry ball,
   He in himself did whole armadoes bring:
Him aged seamen might their master call,
   And choose for general, were he not their king.

XV

It seems as every ship their sovereign knows,
   His awful summons they so soon obey;

So hear the scaly herd when Proteus blows,[d]
  And so to pasture follow thro' the sea.

XVI

To see this fleet upon the ocean move,
  Angels drew wide the curtains of the skies;
And Heav'n, as if there wanted lights above,
  For tapers made two glaring comets rise;

XVII

Whether they unctuous exhalations are,
  Fir'd by the sun, or seeming so alone;
Or each some more remote and slippery star,
  Which loses footing when to mortals shown;

XVIII

Or one, that bright companion of the sun,
  Whose glorious aspect seal'd our new-born king,
And now, a round of greater years begun,
  New influence from his walks of light did bring.

XIX

Victorious York did first, with fam'd success,
  To his known valor make the Dutch give place:
Thus Heav'n our monarch's fortune did confess,
  Beginning conquest from his royal race.

XX

But since it was decreed, auspicious king,
  In Britain's right that thou shouldst wed the main,
Heav'n, as a gage, would cast some precious thing,
  And therefore doom'd that Lawson should be slain.

XXI

Lawson amongst the foremost met his fate,
  Whom sea-green Sirens from the rocks lament:

---

[d]*When Proteus blows* or: *Cœruleus Proteus immania ponti Armenta et magnas pascit sub gurgite phocas.* —VIRGIL.

Thus as an off'ring for the Grecian state,
  He first was kill'd who first to battle went.

XXII

Their chief[e] blown up, in air, not waves, expir'd,
  To which his pride presum'd to give the law:
The Dutch confess'd Heav'n present, and retir'd,
  And all was Britain the wide ocean saw.

XXIII

To nearest ports their shatter'd ships repair,
  Where by our dreadful cannon they lay aw'd:
So reverently men quit the open air,
  When thunder speaks the angry gods abroad.

The Attempt at Berghen

XXIV

And now approach'd their fleet from India, fraught
  With all the riches of the rising sun:
And precious sand from southern climates[f] brought,
  (The fatal regions where the war begun.)

XXV

Like hunted castors, conscious of their store,
  Their waylaid wealth to Norway's coasts they bring:
There first the North's cold bosom spices bore,
  And winter brooded on the eastern spring.

XXVI

By the rich scent we found our perfum'd prey,
  Which, flank'd with rocks, did close in covert lie;
And round about their murdering cannon lay,
  At once to threaten and invite the eye.

XXVII

Fiercer than cannon, and than rocks more hard,
  The English undertake th' unequal war:

---

[e]The Admiral of Holland.
[f]*Southern climates.* Guinea.

Seven ships alone, by which the port is barr'd,
    Besiege the Indies, and all Denmark dare.

XXVIII

These fight like husbands, but like lovers those:
    These fain would keep, and those more fain enjoy;
And to such height their frantic passion grows,
    That what both love, both hazard to destroy.

XXIX

Amidst whole heaps of spices lights a ball,
    And now their odors arm'd against them fly:
Some preciously by shatter'd porc'lain fall,
    And some by aromatic splinters die.

XXX

And tho' by tempests of the prize bereft,
    In heaven's inclemency some ease we find:
Our foes we vanquish'd by our valor left,
    And only yielded to the seas and wind.

XXXI

Nor wholly lost we so deserv'd a prey;
    For storms, repenting, part of it restor'd:
Which, as a tribute from the Baltic sea,
    The British ocean sent her mighty lord.

XXXII

Go, mortals, now, and vex yourselves in vain
    For wealth, which so uncertainly must come:
When what was brought so far, and with such pain,
    Was only kept to lose it nearer home.

XXXIII

The son, who twice three months on th' ocean toss'd,
    Prepar'd to tell what he had pass'd before,
Now sees in English ships the Holland coast,
    And parents' arms in vain stretch'd from the shore.

XXXIV

This careful husband had been long away,
  Whom his chaste wife and little children mourn;
Who on their fingers learn'd to tell the day
  On which their father promis'd to return.

XXXV

Such are the proud designs of humankind,[g]
  And so we suffer ship-wrack everywhere!
Alas, what port can such a pilot find,
  Who in the night of fate must blindly steer!

XXXVI

The undistinguish'd seeds of good and ill,
  Heav'n, in his bosom, from our knowledge hides;
And draws them in contempt of human skill,
  Which oft for friends mistaken foes provides.

XXXVII

Let Munster's prelate ever be accurst,
  In whom we seek the German faith[h] in vain:
Alas, that he should teach the English first,
  That fraud and avarice in the Church could reign!

XXXVIII

Happy, who never trust a stranger's will,
  Whose friendship 's in his interest understood!
Since money giv'n but tempts him to be ill,
  When pow'r is too remote to make him good.

War Declar'd by France

XXXIX

Till now, alone the mighty nations strove;
  The rest, at gaze, without the lists did stand:
And threat'ning France, plac'd like a painted Jove,
  Kept idle thunder in his lifted hand.

---

[g]*Such are*, &c. From Petronius: *Si bene calculum ponas, ubique fit naufragium.*
[h]*The German faith.* Tacitus saith of them: *Nullos mortalium fide aut armis ante Germanos esse.*

XL

That eunuch guardian of rich Holland's trade,
  Who envies us what he wants pow'r t' enjoy;
Whose noiseful valor does no foe invade,
  And weak assistance will his friends destroy:

XLI

Offended that we fought without his leave,
  He takes this time his secret hate to show;
Which Charles does with a mind so calm receive,
  As one that neither seeks nor shuns his foe.

XLII

With France, to aid the Dutch, the Danes unite:
  France as their tyrant, Denmark as their slave.
But when with one three nations join to fight,
  They silently confess that one more brave.

XLIII

Lewis had chas'd the English from his shore,
  But Charles the French as subjects does invite:
Would Heav'n for each some Solomon restore,
  Why, by their mercy, may decide their right!

XLIV

Were subjects so but only by their choice,
  And not from birth did forc'd dominion take,
Our prince alone would have the public voice;
  And all his neighbors' realms would desarts make.

XLV

He without fear a dangerous war pursues,
  Which without rashness he began before:
As honor made him first the danger choose,
  So still he makes it good on virtue's score.

XLVI

The doubled charge his subjects' love supplies,
  Who, in that bounty, to themselves are kind:

So glad Egyptians see their Nilus rise,
  And in his plenty their abundance find.

Prince Rupert and Duke Albemarle Sent to Sea

XLVII

With equal pow'r he does two chiefs create,
  Two such as each seem'd worthiest when alone;
Each able to sustain a nation's fate,
  Since both had found a greater in their own.

XLVIII

Both great in courage, conduct, and in fame,
  Yet neither envious of the other's praise;
Their duty, faith, and int'rest too the same,
  Like mighty partners equally they raise.

XLIX

The prince long time had courted Fortune's love,
  But once possess'd did absolutely reign:
Thus with their Amazons the heroes strove,
  And conquer'd first those beauties they would gain.

L

The duke beheld, like Scipio, with disdain,
  That Carthage which he ruin'd rise once more;
And shook aloft the fasces of the main,
  To fright those slaves with what they felt before.

LI

Together to the wat'ry camp they haste,
  Whom matrons passing to their children show:
Infants' first vows for them to heav'n are cast,
  And future people[i] bless them as they go.

LII

With them no riotous pomp, nor Asian train,
  T' infect a navy with their gaudy fears;

---

[i]*Future people. Examina infantium futurusque populus.* — PLIN. JUN. in *Pan. ad Traj.*

To make slow fights, and victories but vain;
    But war, severely, like itself, appears.

LIII

Diffusive of themselves, where'er they pass,
    They make that warmth in others they expect;
Their valor works like bodies on a glass,
    And does its image on their men project.

Duke of Albemarle's Battle, First Day

LIV

Our fleet divides, and straight the Dutch appear,
    In number, and a fam'd commander, bold:
The narrow seas can scarce their navy bear,
    Or crowded vessels can their soldiers hold.

LV

The duke, less numerous, but in courage more,
    On wings of all the winds to combat flies:
His murdering guns a loud defiance roar,
    And bloody crosses on his flagstaffs rise.

LVI

Both furl their sails, and strip them for the fight,
    Their folded sheets dismiss the useless air:
Th' Elean plains[j] could boast no nobler sight,
    When struggling champions did their bodies bare.

LVII

Borne each by other in a distant line,
    The sea-built forts in dreadful order move:
So vast the noise, as if not fleets did join,
    But lands unfix'd[k] and floating nations strove.

LVIII

Now pass'd, on either side they nimbly tack;
    Both strive to intercept and guide the wind:

---

[j]*Th' Elean*, &c. Where the Olympic games were celebrated.
[k]*Lands unfix'd*, from Virgil: *Credas innare revulsas Cycladas*, &c.

And, in its eye, more closely they come back,
　To finish all the deaths they left behind.

LIX

On high-rais'd decks the haughty Belgians ride,
　Beneath whose shade our humble frigates go:
Such port the elephant bears, and so defied
　By the rhinoceros her unequal foe.

LX

And as the built, so different is the fight;
　Their mounting shot is on our sails design'd;
Deep in their hulls our deadly bullets light,
　And thro' the yielding planks a passage find.

LXI

Our dreaded admiral from far they threat,
　Whose batter'd rigging their whole war receives:
All bare, like some old oak which tempests beat,
　He stands, and sees below his scatter'd leaves.

LXII

Heroes of old, when wounded, shelter sought;
　But he, who meets all danger with disdain,
Ev'n in their face his ship to anchor brought,
　And steeple-high stood propp'd upon the main.

LXIII

At this excess of courage, all amaz'd,
　The foremost of his foes a while withdraw:
With such respect in enter'd Rome they gaz'd,
　Who on high chairs the godlike fathers saw.

LXIV

And now, as where Patroclus' body lay,
　Here Trojan chiefs advanc'd, and there the Greek;
Ours o'er the duke their pious wings display,
　And theirs the noblest spoils of Britain seek.

LXV

Meantime his busy mariners he hastes,
  His shatter'd sails with rigging to restore;
And willing pines ascend his broken masts,
  Whose lofty heads rise higher than before.

LXVI

Straight to the Dutch he turns his dreadful prow,
  More fierce th' important quarrel to decide:
Like swans, in long array his vessels show,
  Whose crests, advancing, do the waves divide.

LXVII

They charge, recharge, and all along the sea
  They drive, and squander the huge Belgian fleet.
Berkeley alone, who nearest danger lay,
  Did a like fate with lost Creüsa meet.

LXVIII

The night comes on, we eager to pursue
  The combat still, and they asham'd to leave:
Till the last streaks of dying day withdrew,
  And doubtful moonlight did our rage deceive.

LXIX

In th' English fleet each ship resounds with joy,
  And loud applause of their great leader's fame:
In fiery dreams the Dutch they still destroy,
  And, slumb'ring, smile at the imagin'd flame.

LXX

Not so the Holland fleet, who, tir'd and done,
  Stretch'd on their decks like weary oxen lie:
Faint sweats all down their mighty members run,
  (Vast bulks, which little souls but ill supply.)

LXXI

In dreams they fearful precipices tread;
  Or, ship-wrack'd, labor to some distant shore:

Or in dark churches walk among the dead;
   They wake with horror, and dare sleep no more.

Second Day's Battle

LXXII

The morn they look on with unwilling eyes,
   Till from their maintop joyful news they hear
Of ships, which by their mold bring new supplies,
   And in their colors Belgian lions bear.

LXXIII

Our watchful general had discern'd from far
   This mighty succor, which made glad the foe;
He sigh'd, but, like a father of the war,
   His face spake hope, while deep his sorrows flow.[1]

LXXIV

His wounded men he first sends off to shore,
   (Never, till now, unwilling to obey:)
They not their wounds, but want of strength deplore,
   And think them happy who with him can stay.

LXXV

Then to the rest: "Rejoice," said he, "to-day;
   In you the fortune of Great Britain lies:
Among so brave a people, you are they
   Whom Heav'n has chose to fight for such a prize.

LXXVI

"If number English courages could quell,
   We should at first have shunn'd, not met, our foes,
Whose numerous sails the fearful only tell:
   Courage from hearts, and not from numbers, grows."

LXXVII

He said, nor needed more to say: with haste
   To their known stations cheerfully they go;

---

[1]*His face, &c. Spem vultu simulat, premit alto corde dolorem.* —VIRGIL.

And all at once, disdaining to be last,
  Solicit every gale to meet the foe.

LXXVIII

Nor did th' incourag'd Belgians long delay,
  But bold in others, not themselves, they stood:
So thick, our navy scarce could steer their way,
  But seem'd to wander in a moving wood.

LXXIX

Our little fleet was now ingag'd so far,
  That, like the swordfish in the whale, they fought:
The combat only seem'd a civil war,
  Till thro' their bowels we our passage wrought.

LXXX

Never had valor, no, not ours, before
  Done aught like this upon the land or main,
Where not to be o'ercome was to do more
  Than all the conquests former kings did gain.

LXXXI

The mighty ghosts of our great Harries rose,
  And armed Edwards look'd, with anxious eyes,
To see this fleet among unequal foes,
  By which fate promis'd them their Charles should rise.

LXXXII

Meantime the Belgians tack upon our rear,
  And raking chase-guns thro' our sterns they send:
Close by, their fire-ships, like jackals, appear,
  Who on their lions for the prey attend.

LXXXIII

Silent in smoke of cannons they come on:
  (Such vapors once did fiery Cacus hide:)
In these the height of pleas'd revenge is shown,
  Who burn contented by another's side.

LXXXIV

Sometimes, from fighting squadrons of each fleet,
   (Deceiv'd themselves, or to preserve some friend,)
Two grappling Ætnas on the ocean meet,
   And English fires with Belgian flames contend.

LXXXV

Now, at each tack, our little fleet grows less;
   And, like maim'd fowl, swim lagging on the main;
Their greater loss their numbers scarce confess,
   While they lose cheaper than the English gain.

LXXXVI

Have you not seen, when, whistled from the fist,
   Some falcon stoops at what her eye design'd,
And, with her eagerness the quarry miss'd,
   Straight flies at check, and clips it down the wind;

LXXXVII

The dastard crow, that to the wood made wing,
   And sees the groves no shelter can afford,
With her loud caws her craven kind does bring,
   Who, safe in numbers, cuff the noble bird?

LXXXVIII

Among the Dutch thus Albemarle did fare:
   He could not conquer, and disdain'd to fly;
Past hope of safety, 't was his latest care,
   Like falling Cæsar, decently to die.

LXXXIX

Yet pity did his manly spirit move,
   To see those perish who so well had fought;
And generously with his despair he strove,
   Resolv'd to live till he their safety wrought.

XC

Let other Muses write his prosp'rous fate,
   Of conquer'd nations tell, and kings restor'd;

But mine shall sing of his eclips'd estate,
    Which, like the sun's, more wonders does afford.

XCI

He drew his mighty frigates all before,
    On which the foe his fruitless force employs:
His weak ones deep into his rear he bore,
    Remote from guns, as sick men from the noise.

XCII

His fiery cannon did their passage guide,
    And foll'wing smoke obscur'd them from the foe:
Thus Israel safe from the Egyptian's pride,
    By flaming pillars, and by clouds did go.

XCIII

Elsewhere the Belgian force we did defeat,
    But here our courages did theirs subdue;
So Xenophon once led that fam'd retreat,
    Which first the Asian empire overthrew.

XCIV

The foe approach'd; and one, for his bold sin,
    Was sunk; (as he that touch'd the ark was slain:)
The wild waves master'd him and suck'd him in,
    And smiling eddies dimpled on the main.

XCV

This seen, the rest at awful distance stood;
    As if they had been there as servants set,
To stay, or to go on, as he thought good,
    And not pursue, but wait on his retreat.

XCVI

So Libyan huntsmen, on some sandy plain,
    From shady coverts rous'd, the lion chase:
The kingly beast roars out with loud disdain,
    And slowly moves, unknowing to give place.[m]

---

[m]The simile is Virgil's: *Vestigia retro improperata refert*, &c.

XCVII

But if some one approach to dare his force,
   He swings his tail, and swiftly turns him round;
With one paw seizes on his trembling horse,
   And with the other tears him to the ground.

XCVIII

Amidst these toils succeeds the balmy night;
   Now hissing waters the quench'd guns restore;
And weary waves,[n] withdrawing from the fight,
   Lie lull'd and panting on the silent shore.

XCIX

The moon shone clear on the becalmed flood,
   Where, while her beams like glittering silver play,
Upon the deck our careful general stood,
   And deeply mus'd on the succeeding day.[o]

C

"That happy sun," said he, "will rise again,
   Who twice victorious did our navy see;
And I alone must view him rise in vain,
   Without one ray of all his star for me.

CI

"Yet like an English gen'ral will I die,
   And all the ocean make my spacious grave:
Women and cowards on the land may lie;
   The sea 's a tomb that 's proper for the brave."

CII

Restless he pass'd the remnants of the night,
   Till the fresh air proclam'd the morning nigh;
And burning ships, the martyrs of the fight,
   With paler fires beheld the eastern sky.

---

[n]*Weary waves:* from Statius, *Sylvæ: Nec trucibus fluviis idem sonus: occidit horror Æquoris, antennis maria acclinata quiescunt.*
[o]The third of June, famous for two former victories.

Third Day

CIII

But now, his stores of ammunition spent,
　　His naked valor is his only guard;
Rare thunders are from his dumb cannon sent,
　　And solitary guns are scarcely heard.

CIV

Thus far had Fortune pow'r, here forc'd to stay,
　　Nor longer durst with virtue be at strife:
This, as a ransom, Albemarle did pay
　　For all the glories of so great a life.

CV

For now brave Rupert from afar appears,
　　Whose waving streamers the glad general knows:
With full-spread sails his eager navy steers,
　　And every ship in swift proportion grows.

CVI

The anxious prince had heard the cannon long,
　　And from that length of time dire omens drew
Of English overmatch'd, and Dutch too strong,
　　Who never fought three days, but to pursue.

CVII

Then, as an eagle, who with pious care
　　Was beating widely on the wing for prey,
To her now silent eyry does repair,
　　And finds her callow infants forc'd away;

CVIII

Stung with her love, she stoops upon the plain,
　　The broken air loud whistling as she flies,
She stops and listens, and shoots forth again,
　　And guides her pinions by her young ones' cries:

CIX

With such kind passion hastes the prince to fight,
  And spreads his flying canvas to the sound;
Him, whom no danger, were he there, could fright,
  Now, absent, every little noise can wound.

CX

As in a drought the thirsty creatures cry,
  And gape upon the gather'd clouds for rain;
And first the martlet meets it in the sky,
  And with wet wings joys all the feather'd train.

CXI

With such glad hearts did our despairing men
  Salute th' appearance of the prince's fleet;
And each ambitiously would claim the ken
  That with first eyes did distant safety meet.

CXII

The Dutch, who came like greedy hinds before,
  To reap the harvest their ripe ears did yield;
Now look like those, when rolling thunders roar,
  And sheets of lightning blast the standing field.

CXIII

Full in the prince's passage, hills of sand
  And dang'rous flats in secret ambush lay,
Where the false tides skim o'er the cover'd land,
  And seamen with dissembled depths betray.

CXIV

The wily Dutch, who, like fall'n angels, fear'd
  This new Messiah's coming, there did wait,
And round the verge their braving vessels steer'd,
  To tempt his courage with so fair a bait.

CXV

But he, unmov'd, contemns their idle threat,
  Secure of fame whene'er he please to fight:

His cold experience tempers all his heat,
    And inbred worth doth boasting valor slight.

CXVI

Heroic virtue did his actions guide,
    And he the substance, not the appearance chose;
To rescue one such friend he took more pride
    Than to destroy whole thousands of such foes.

CXVII

But when approach'd, in strict embraces bound,
    Rupert and Albemarle together grow;
He joys to have his friend in safety found,
    Which he to none but to that friend would owe.

CXVIII

The cheerful soldiers, with new stores supplied,
    Now long to execute their spleenful will;
And in revenge for those three days they tried,
    Wish one, like Joshua's, when the sun stood still.

Fourth Day's Battle

CXIX

Thus reinforc'd, against the adverse fleet,
    Still doubling ours, brave Rupert leads the way:
With the first blushes of the morn they meet,
    And bring night back upon the new-born day.

CXX

His presence soon blows up the kindling fight,
    And his loud guns speak thick like angry men:
It seem'd as slaughter had been breath'd all night,
    And Death new pointed his dull dart again.

CXXI

The Dutch too well his mighty conduct knew,
    And matchless courage, since the former fight:
Whose navy like a stiff-stretch'd cord did shew,
    Till he bore in and bent them into flight.

CXXII

The wind he shares, while half their fleet offends
    His open side, and high above him shows:
Upon the rest at pleasure he descends,
    And, doubly harm'd, he double harms bestows.

CXXIII

Behind, the gen'ral mends his weary pace
    And sullenly to his revenge he sails;
So glides some trodden serpent on the grass,
    And long behind his wounded volume trails.[p]

CXXIV

Th' increasing sound is borne to either shore,
    And for their stakes the throwing nations fear:
Their passion double with the cannons' roar,
    And with warm wishes each man combats there.

CXXV

Plied thick and close as when the fight begun,
    Their huge unwieldy navy wastes away;
So sicken waning moons too near the sun,
    And blunt their crescents on the edge of day.

CXXVI

And now reduc'd on equal terms to fight,
    Their ships like wasted patrimonies show;
Where the thin scatt'ring trees admit the light,
    And shun each other's shadows as they grow.

CXXVII

The warlike prince had sever'd from the rest
    Two giant ships, the pride of all the main;
Which with his one so vigorously he press'd,
    And flew so home they could not rise again.

---

[p]So glides, &c. From Virgil: *Quum medii nexus, extremœque agmina caudœ Solvuntur; tardosque trahit sinus ultimus orbes,* &c.

CXXVIII

Already batter'd, by his lee they lay;
  In vain upon the passing winds they call:
The passing winds thro' their torn canvas play,
  And flagging sails on heartless sailors fall.

CXXIX

Their open'd sides receive a gloomy light,
  Dreadful as day let in to shades below;
Without, grim Death rides barefac'd in their sight,
And urges ent'ring billows as they flow.

CXXX

When one dire shot, the last they could supply,
  Close by the board the prince's mainmast bore:
All three now, helpless, by each other lie,
  And this offends not, and those fear no more.

CXXXI

So have I seen some fearful hare maintain
  A course, till tir'd before the dog she lay;
Who, stretch'd behind her, pants upon the plain,
  Past pow'r to kill, as she to get away:

CXXXII

With his loll'd tongue he faintly licks his prey;
  His warm breath blows her flix up as she lies;
She, trembling, creeps upon the ground away,
  And looks back to him with beseeching eyes.

CXXXIII

The prince unjustly does his stars accuse,
  Which hinder'd him to push his fortune on;
For what they to his courage did refuse,
  By mortal valor never must be done.

CXXXIV

This lucky hour the wise Batavian takes,
  And warns his tatter'd fleet to follow home:

Proud to have so got off with equal stakes,
   Where 't was a triumph not to be o'ercome.[q]

CXXXV

The general's force, as kept alive by fight,
   Now, not oppos'd, no longer can pursue:
Lasting till Heav'n had done his courage right;
   When he had conquer'd, he his weakness knew.

CXXXVI

He casts a frown on the departing foe,
   And sighs to see him quit the wat'ry field:
His stern fix'd eyes no satisfaction show
   For all the glories which the fight did yield.

CXXXVII

Tho', as when fiends did miracles avow,
   He stands confess'd ev'n by the boastful Dutch;
He only does his conquest disavow,
   And thinks too little what they found too much.

CXXXVIII

Return'd, he with the fleet resolv'd to stay;
   No tender thoughts of home his heart divide;
Domestic joys and cares he puts away;
   For realms are households which the great must guide.

CXXXIX

As those who unripe veins in mines explore,
   On the rich bed again the warm turf lay,
Till time digests the yet imperfect ore,
   And know it will be gold another day:

CXL

So looks our monarch on this early fight,
   Th' essay and rudiments of great success;
Which all-maturing time must bring to light,
   While he, like Heav'n, does each day's labor bless.

---

[q]From Horace: *Quos opimus Fallere et effugere est triumphus.*

CXLI

Heav'n ended not the first or second day,
　　Yet each was perfect to the work design'd:
God and kings work, when they their work survey,
　　And passive aptness in all subjects find.

His Majesty Repairs the Fleet

CXLII

In burden'd vessels first, with speedy care,
　　His plenteous stores do season'd timber send:
Thither the brawny carpenters repair,
　　And as the surgeons of maim'd ships attend.

CXLIII

With cord and canvas from rich Hamburg sent,
　　IIis navies' molted wings he imps once more;
Tall Norway fir, their masts in battle spent,
　　And English oak, sprung leaks and planks, restore.

CXLIV

All hands employ'd, the royal work grows warm:[r]
　　Like laboring bees on a long summer's day,
Some sound the trumpet for the rest to swarm,
　　And some on bells of tasted lilies play;

CXLV

With gluey wax some new foundations lay
　　Of virgin combs, which from the roof are hung;
Some arm'd within doors upon duty stay,
　　Or tend the sick, or educate the young.

CXLVI

So here, some pick out bullets from the sides,
　　Some drive old oakum thro' each seam and rift:
Their left hand does the calking-iron guide,
　　The rattling mallet with the right they lift.

---

[r]*Fervet opus:* the same similitude in Virgil.

CXLVII

With boiling pitch another near at hand,
  From friendly Sweden brought, the seams instops:
Which well paid o'er, the salt sea waves withstand,
  And shakes them from the rising beak in drops.

CXLVIII

Some the gall'd ropes with dauby marling bind,
  Or searcloth masts with strong tarpauling coats:
To try new shrouds one mounts into the wind,
  And one, below, their ease or stiffness notes.

CXLIX

Our careful monarch stands in person by,
  His new-cast cannons' firmness to explore:
The strength of big-corn'd powder loves to try,
  And ball and cartrage sorts for every bore.

CL

Each day brings fresh supplies of arms and men,
  And ships which all last winter were abroad;
And such as fitted since the fight had been,
  Or new from stocks were fall'n into the road.

Loyal London Describ'd

CLI

The goodly London in her gallant trim,
  (The Phœnix daughter of the vanish'd old,)
Like a rich bride does to the ocean swim,
  And on her shadow rides in floating gold.

CLII

Her flag aloft, spread ruffling to the wind,
  And sanguine streamers seem the flood to fire:
The weaver, charm'd with what his loom design'd,
  Goes on to sea, and knows not to retire.

CLIII

With roomy decks, her guns of mighty strength,
    Whose low-laid mouths each mounting billow laves:
Deep in her draught, and warlike in her length,
    She seems a sea-wasp flying on the waves.

CLIV

This martial present, piously design'd,
    The loyal city give their best-lov'd king:
And, with a bounty ample as the wind,
    Built, fitted, and maintain'd, to aid him bring.

Digression Concerning Shipping and Navigation

CLV

By viewing Nature, Nature's handmaid Art
    Makes mighty things from small beginnings grow:
Thus fishes first to shipping did impart
    Their tail the rudder, and their head the prow.

CLVI

Some log, perhaps, upon the waters swam,
    An useless drift, which, rudely cut within,
And hollow'd, first a floating trough became,
    And cross some riv'let passage did begin.

CLVII

In shipping such as this, the Irish kern,
    And untaught Indian, on the stream did glide:
Ere sharp-keel'd boats to stem the flood did learn,
    Or fin-like oars did spread from either side.

CLVIII

Add but a sail, and Saturn so appear'd,
    When from lost empire he to exile went,
And with the golden age to Tiber steer'd,
    Where coin and first commerce he did invent.

CLIX

Rude as their ships was navigation then;
  No useful compass or meridian known;
Coasting, they kept the land within their ken,
  And knew no North but when the Pole-star shone.

CLX

Of all who since have us'd the open sea,
  Than the bold English none more fame have won;
Beyond the year, and out of heav'n's high way,[s]
  They make discoveries where they see no sun.

CLXI

But what so long in vain, and yet unknown,
  By poor mankind's benighted wit is sought,
Shall in this age to Britain first be shown,
  And hence be to admiring nations taught.

CLXII

The ebbs of tides and their mysterious flow,
  We, as arts' elements, shall understand,
And as by line upon the ocean go,
  Whose paths shall be familiar as the land.

CLXIII

Instructed ships shall sail to quick commerce,[t]
  By which remotest regions are allied;
Which makes one city of the universe;
  Where some may gain, and all may be supplied.

CLXIV

Then, we upon our globe's last verge shall go,
  And view the ocean leaning on the sky:
From thence our rolling neighbors we shall know,
  And on the lunar world securely pry.

---

[s]*Extra anni solisque vias.* —VIRG.
[t]By a more exact measure of longitude.

Apostrophe to the Royal Society

CLXV

This I foretell from your auspicious care,
    Who great in search of God and Nature grow;
Who best your wise Creator's praise declare,
    Since best to praise his works is best to know.

CLXVI

O truly Royal! who behold the law
    And rule of beings in your Maker's mind;
And thence, like limbecs, rich ideas draw,
    To fit the level'd use of humankind.

CLXVII

But first the toils of war we must endure,
    And from th' injurious Dutch redeem the seas.
War makes the valiant of his right secure,
    And gives up fraud to be chastis'd with ease.

CLXVIII

Already were the Belgians on our coast,
    Whose fleet more mighty every day became
By late success, which they did falsely boast,
    And now by first appearing seem'd to claim.

CLXIX

Designing, subtile, diligent, and close,
    They knew to manage war with wise delay:
Yet all those arts their vanity did cross,
    And, by their pride, their prudence did betray.

CLXX

Nor stay'd the English long; but, well supplied,
    Appear as numerous as th' insulting foe:
The combat now by courage must be tried,
    And the success the braver nation show.

CLXXI

There was the Plymouth squadron now come in,
  Which in the Straits last winter was abroad;
Which twice on Biscay's working bay had been,
  And on the midland sea the French had aw'd.

CLXXII

Old expert Allen, loyal all along,
  Fam'd for his action on the Smyrna fleet;
And Holmes, whose name shall live in epic song,
  While music numbers, or while verse has feet;

CLXXIII

Holmes, the Achates of the gen'rals' fight,
  Who first bewitch'd our eyes with Guinea gold,
As once old Cato in the Romans' sight
  The tempting fruits of Afric did unfold.

CLXXIV

With him went Sprag, as bountiful as brave,
  Whom his high courage to command had brought;
Harman, who did the twice-fir'd Harry save,
  And in his burning ship undaunted fought;

CLXXV

Young Hollis, on a Muse by Mars begot,
  Born, Cæsar-like, to write and act great deeds:
Impatient to revenge his fatal shot,
  His right hand doubly to his left succeeds.

CLXXVI

Thousands were there in darker fame that dwell,
  Whose deeds some nobler poem shall adorn;
And tho' to me unknown, they, sure, fought well,
  Whom Rupert led, and who were British born.

CLXXVII

Of every size an hundred fighting sail,
  So vast the navy now at anchor rides,

That underneath it the press'd waters fail,
    And with its weight it shoulders off the tides.

CLXXVIII

Now, anchors weigh'd, the seamen shout so shrill,
    That heav'n, and earth, and the wide ocean rings;
A breeze from westward waits their sails to fill,
    And rests in those high beds his downy wings.

CLXXIX

The wary Dutch this gathering storm foresaw,
    And durst not bide it on the English coast:
Behind their treach'rous shallows they withdraw,
    And there lay snares to catch the British host.

CLXXX

So the false spider, when her nets are spread,
    Deep ambush'd in her silent den does lie,
And feels far off the trembling of her thread,
    Whose filmy cord should bind the struggling fly;

CLXXXI

Then, if at last she find him fast beset,
    She issues forth, and runs along her loom:
She joys to touch the captive in her net,
    And drags the little wretch in triumph home.

CLXXXII

The Belgians hop'd that, with disorder'd haste,
    Our deep-cut keels upon the sands might run;
Or, if with caution leisurely were pass'd,
    Their numerous gross might charge us one by one.

CLXXXIII

But with a fore-wind pushing them above,
    And swelling tide that heav'd them from below,
O'er the blind flats our warlike squadrons move,
    And with spread sails to welcome battle go.

CLXXXIV

It seem'd as there the British Neptune stood,
    With all his hosts of waters at command,
Beneath them to submit th' officious flood,
    And with his trident shov'd them off the sand.[u]

CLXXXV

To the pale foes they suddenly draw near,
    And summon them to unexpected fight;
They start like murderers when ghosts appear,
    And draw their curtains in the dead of night.

Second Battle

CLXXXVI

Now van to van the foremost squadrons meet,
    The midmost battles hast'ning up behind;
Who view, far off, the storm of falling sleet,
    And hear their thunder rattling in the wind.

CLXXXVII

At length the adverse admirals appear;
    (The two bold champions of each country's right:)
Their eyes describe the lists as they come near,
    And draw the lines of death before they fight.

CLXXXVIII

The distance judg'd for shot of every size,
    The linstocks touch, the pond'rous ball expires:
The vig'rous seaman every porthole plies,
    And adds his heart to every gun he fires.

CLXXXIX

Fierce was the fight on the proud Belgians' side,
    For honor, which they seldom sought before;
But now they by their own vain boasts were tied,
    And forc'd at least in shew to prize it more.

---

[u]*Levat ipse tridenti, Et vastas aperit syrtes,* &c.—VIRG.

CXC

But sharp remembrance on the English part,
　And shame of being match'd by such a foe,
Rouse conscious virtue up in every heart,
　And seeming to be stronger makes them so.[v]

CXCI

Nor long the Belgians could that fleet sustain,
　Which did two gen'rals' fates, and Cæsar's bear:
Each several ship a victory did gain,
　As Rupert or as Albemarle were there.

CXCII

Their batter'd admiral too soon withdrew,
　Unthank'd by ours for his unfinish'd fight;
But he the minds of his Dutch masters knew,
　Who call'd that providence which we call'd flight.

CXCIII

Never did men more joyfully obey,
　Or sooner understood the sign to fly:
With such alacrity they bore away,
　As if to praise them all the States stood by.

CXCIV

O famous leader of the Belgian fleet,
　Thy monument inscrib'd such praise shall wear,
As Varro, timely flying, once did meet,
　Because he did not of his Rome despair.

CXCV

Behold that navy, which a while before
　Provok'd the tardy English close to fight,
Now draw their beaten vessels close to shore,
　As larks lie dar'd to shun the hobby's flight.

---

[v]*Possunt, quia posse videntur.* —Virg.

CXCVI

Whoe'er would English monuments survey,
    In other records may our courage know:
But let them hide the story of this day,
    Whose fame was blemish'd by too base a foe.

CXCVII

Or if too busily they will enquire
    Into a victory which we disdain;
Then let them know, the Belgians did retire
    Before the patron saint[w] of injur'd Spain.

CXCVIII

Repenting England this revengeful day
    To Philip's manes[x] did an off'ring bring:
England, which first, by leading them astray,
    Hatch'd up rebellion to destroy her king.

CXCIX

Our fathers bent their baneful industry
    To check a monarchy that slowly grew;
But did not France or Holland's fate foresee,
    Whose rising pow'r to swift dominion flew.

CC

In fortune's empire blindly thus we go,
    And wander after pathless destiny;
Whose dark resorts since prudence cannot know,
    In vain it would provide for what shall be.

CCI

But whate'er English to the blest shall go,
    And the fourth Harry or first Orange meet;
Find him disowning of a Burbon foe,
    And him detesting a Batavian fleet.

---

[w]*Patron saint:* St. James, on whose day this victory was gain'd.
[x]*Philip's manes:* Philip the Second of Spain, against whom the Hollanders, rebelling, were aided by Queen Elizabeth.

CCII

Now on their coasts our conquering navy rides,
  Waylays their merchants, and their land besets;
Each day new wealth without their care provides;
  They lie asleep with prizes in their nets.

CCIII

So, close behind some promontory lie
  The huge leviathans t' attend their prey;
And give no chase, but swallow in the fry,
  Which thro' their gaping jaws mistake the way.

Burning of the Fleet in the Vlie by Sir Robert Holmes

CCIV

Nor was this all: in ports and roads remote,
  Destructive fires among whole fleets we send;
Triumphant flames upon the water float,
  And outbound ships at home their voyage end.

CCV

Those various squadrons, variously design'd,
  Each vessel freighted with a several load,
Each squadron waiting for a several wind,
  All find but one, to burn them in the road.

CCVI

Some bound for Guinea, golden sand to find,
  Bore all the gauds the simple natives wear;
Some, for the pride of Turkish courts design'd,
  For folded turbants finest Holland bear.

CCVII

Some English wool, vex'd in a Belgian loom,
  And into cloth of spongy softness made,
Did into France or colder Denmark doom,
  To ruin with worse ware our staple trade.

CCVIII

Our greedy seamen rummage every hold,
  Smile on the booty of each wealthier chest;
And, as the priests who with their gods make bold,
  Take what they like, and sacrifice the rest.

Transit to the Fire of London

CCIX

But ah! how unsincere are all our joys!
  Which, sent from heav'n, like lightning make no stay:
Their palling taste the journey's length destroys,
  Or grief, sent post, o'ertakes them on the way.

CCX

Swell'd with our late successes on the foe,
  Which France and Holland wanted power to cross,
We urge an unseen fate to lay us low,
  And feed their envious eyes with English loss.

CCXI

Each element his dread command obeys,
  Who makes or ruins with a smile or frown;
Who, as by one he did our nation raise,
  So now he with another pulls us down.

CCXII

Yet London, empress of the northern clime,
  By an high fate thou greatly didst expire:
Great as the world's, which at the death of time
  Must fall, and rise a nobler frame by fire.[y]

CCXIII

As when some dire usurper Heav'n provides
  To scourge his country with a lawless sway,
His birth perhaps some petty village hides,
  And sets his cradle out of fortune's way,

---

[y]*Quum mare, quum tellus correptaque regia cœli Ardeat,* &c. — OVID.

CCXIV

Till fully ripe his swelling fate breaks out,
    And hurries him to mighty mischiefs on;
His prince, surpris'd at first, no ill could doubt,
    And wants the pow'r to meet it when 't is known.

CCXV

Such was the rise of this prodigious fire,
    Which, in mean buildings first obscurely bred,
From thence did soon to open streets aspire,
    And straight to palaces and temples spread.

CCXVI

The diligence of trades and noiseful gain,
    And luxury, more late, asleep were laid:
All was the Night's, and in her silent reign
    No sound the rest of nature did invade.

CCXVII

In this deep quiet, from what source unknown,
    Those seeds of fire their fatal birth disclose;
And first, few scatt'ring sparks about were blown,
    Big with the flames that to our ruin rose.

CCXVIII

Then, in some close-pent room it crept along,
    And, smould'ring as it went, in silence fed;
Till th' infant monster, with devouring strong,
    Walk'd boldly upright with exalted head.

CCXIX

Now, like some rich or mighty murderer,
    Too great for prison, which he breaks with gold;
Who fresher for new mischiefs does appear,
    And dares the world to tax him with the old;

CCXX

So scapes th' insulting fire his narrow jail,
    And makes small outlets into open air;

There the fierce winds his tender force assail,
    And beat him downward to his first repair.

CCXXI

The winds, like crafty courtesans, withheld
    His flames from burning, but to blow them more:ᶻ
And, every fresh attempt, he is repell'd
    With faint denials, weaker than before.

CCXXII

And now, no longer letted of his prey,
    He leaps up at it with inrag'd desire;
O'erlooks the neighbors with a wide survey,
    And nods at every house his threat'ning fire.

CCXXIII

The ghosts of traitors from the Bridge descend,
    With bold fanatic specters to rejoice;
About the fire into a dance they bend,
    And sing their sabbath notes with feeble voice.

CCXXIV

Our guardian angel saw them where he sate
    Above the palace of our slumb'ring king:
He sigh'd, abandoning his charge to fate,
    And, drooping, oft look'd back upon the wing.

CCXXV

At length the crackling noise and dreadful blaze
    Call'd up some waking lover to the sight;
And long it was ere he the rest could raise,
    Whose heavy eyelids yet were full of night.

CCXXVI

The next to danger, hot pursued by fate,
    Half-cloth'd, half-naked, hastily retire;
And frighted mothers strike their breasts, too late,
    For helpless infants left amidst the fire.

ᶻ*Like crafty*, &c. *Hæc arte tractabat cupidum virum, ut illius animum inopia accenderet.*

CCXXVII

Their cries soon waken all the dwellers near;
    Now murmuring noises rise in every street;
The more remote run stumbling with their fear,
    And in the dark men justle as they meet.

CCXXVIII

So weary bees in little cells repose;
    But if night-robbers lift the well-stor'd hive,
An humming thro' their waxen city grows,
    And out upon each other's wings they drive.

CCXXIX

Now streets grow throng'd and busy as by day:
    Some run for buckets to the hallow'd choir:
Some cut the pipes, and some the engines play;
    And some more bold mount ladders to the fire.

CCXXX

In vain; for from the East a Belgian wind
    His hostile breath thro' the dry rafters sent;
The flames impell'd soon left their foes behind,
    And forward with a wanton fury went.

CCXXXI

A key of fire ran all along the shore,
    And lighten'd all the river with a blaze;[a]
The waken'd tides began again to roar,
    And wond'ring fish in shining waters gaze.

CCXXXII

Old father Thames rais'd up his reverend head,
    But fear'd the fate of Simoeis would return:
Deep in his ooze he sought his sedgy bed,
    And shrunk his waters back into his urn.

---

[a]*Sigœa igni freta lata relucent.* —VIRG.

CCXXXIII

The fire, meantime, walks in a broader gross;
  To either hand his wings he opens wide:
He wades the streets, and straight he reaches cross,
  And plays his longing flames on th' other side.

CCXXXIV

At first they warm, then scorch, and then they take;
  Now with long necks from side to side they feed;
At length, grown strong, their mother-fire forsake,
  And a new colony of flames succeed.

CCXXXV

To every nobler portion of the town
  The curling billows roll their restless tide:
In parties now they straggle up and down,
  As armies, unoppos'd, for prey divide.

CCXXXVI

One mighty squadron, with a side-wind sped,
  Thro' narrow lanes his cumber'd fire does haste,
By pow'rful charms of gold and silver led,
  The Lombard bankers and the Change to waste.

CCXXXVII

Another backward to the Tow'r would go,
  And slowly eats his way against the wind;
But the main body of the marching foe
  Against th' imperial palace is design'd.

CCXXXVIII

Now day appears, and with the day the king,
  Whose early care had robb'd him of his rest:
Far off the cracks of falling houses ring,
  And shrieks of subjects pierce his tender breast.

CCXXXIX

Near as he draws, thick harbingers of smoke
  With gloomy pillars cover all the place;

Whose little intervals of night are broke
  By sparks that drive against his sacred face.

CCXL

More than his guards his sorrows made him known,
  And pious tears, which down his cheeks did show'r:
The wretched in his grief forgot their own;
  (So much the pity of a king has pow'r.)

CCXLI

He wept the flames of what he lov'd so well,
  And what so well had merited his love:
For never prince in grace did more excel,
  Or royal city more in duty strove.

CCXLII

Nor with an idle care did he behold:
  (Subjects may grieve, but monarchs must redress;)
He cheers the fearful, and commends the bold,
  And makes despairers hope for good success.

CCXLIII

Himself directs what first is to be done,
  And orders all the succors which they bring:
The helpful and the good about him run,
  And form an army worthy such a king.

CCXLIV

He sees the dire contagion spread so fast,
  That, where it seizes, all relief is vain;
And therefore must unwillingly lay waste
  That country which would, else, the foe maintain.

CCXLV

The powder blows up all before the fire:
  Th' amazed flames stand gather'd on a heap;
And from the precipice's brink retire,
  Afraid to venture on so large a leap.

CCXLVI

Thus fighting fires a while themselves consume,
  But straight, like Turks, forc'd on to win or die,
They first lay tender bridges of their fume,
  And o'er the breach in unctuous vapors fly.

CCXLVII

Part stays for passage, till a gust of wind
  Ships o'er their forces in a shining sheet:
Part, creeping under ground, their journey blind,
  And, climbing from below, their fellows meet.

CCXLVIII

Thus to some desert plain, or old wood-side,
  Dire night-hags come from far to dance their round;
And o'er broad rivers on their fiends they ride,
  Or sweep in clouds above the blasted ground.

CCXLIX

No help avails: for, hydra-like, the fire
  Lifts up his hundred heads to aim his way;
And scarce the wealthy can one half retire,
  Before he rushes in to share the prey.

CCL

The rich grow suppliant, and the poor grow proud;
  Those offer mighty gain, and these ask more:
So void of pity is th' ignoble crowd,
  When others' ruin may increase their store.

CCLI

As those who live by shores with joy behold
  Some wealthy vessel split or stranded nigh,
And from the rocks leap down for ship-wrack'd gold,
  And seek the tempests which the others fly:

CCLII

So these but wait the owners' last despair,
  And what 's permitted to the flames invade:

Ev'n from their jaws they hungry morsels tear,
    And on their backs the spoils of Vulcan lade.

CCLIII

The days were all in this lost labor spent;
    And when the weary king gave place to night,
His beams he to his royal brother lent,
    And so shone still in his reflective light.

CCLIV

Night came, but without darkness or repose,
    A dismal picture of the gen'ral doom;
Where souls distracted, when the trumpet blows,
    And half unready with their bodies come.

CCLV

Those who have homes, when home they do repair,
    To a last lodging call their wand'ring friends:
Their short uneasy sleeps are broke with care,
    To look how near their own destruction tends.

CCLVI

Those who have none, sit round where once it was,
    And with full eyes each wonted room require;
Haunting the yet warm ashes of the place,
    As murder'd men walk where they did expire.

CCLVII

Some stir up coals, and watch the vestal fire,
    Others in vain from sight of ruin run;
And, while thro' burning lab'rinths they retire,
    With loathing eyes repeat what they would shun.

CCLVIII

The most in fields like herded beasts lie down,
    To dews obnoxious on the grassy floor;
And while their babes in sleep their sorrows drown,
    Sad parents watch the remnants of their store.

CCLIX

While by the motion of the flames they guess
  What streets are burning now, and what are near,
An infant, waking, to the paps would press,
  And meets, instead of milk, a falling tear.

CCLX

No thought can ease them but their sovereign's care,
  Whose praise th' afflicted as their comfort sing:
Ev'n those whom want might drive to just despair,
  Think life a blessing under such a king.

CCLXI

Meantime he sadly suffers in their grief,
  Out-weeps an hermit, and out-prays a saint:
All the long night he studies their relief,
  How they may be supplied, and he may want.

King's Prayer

CCLXII

"O God," said he, "thou patron of my days,
  Guide of my youth in exile and distress!
Who me unfriended brought'st by wondrous ways,
  The kingdom of my fathers to possess:

CCLXIII

"Be thou my judge, with what unwearied care
  I since have labor'd for my people's good;
To bind the bruises of a civil war,
  And stop the issues of their wasting blood.

CCLXIV

"Thou, who hast taught me to forgive the ill,
  And recompense, as friends, the good misled;
If mercy be a precept of thy will,
  Return that mercy on thy servant's head.

CCLXV

"Or, if my heedless youth has stepp'd astray,
   Too soon forgetful of thy gracious hand;
On me alone thy just displeasure lay,
   But take thy judgments from this mourning land.

CCLXVI

"We all have sinn'd, and thou hast laid us low,
   As humble earth from whence at first we came:
Like flying shades before the clouds we show,
   And shrink like parchment in consuming flame.

CCLXVII

"O let it be enough what thou hast done;
   When spotted deaths ran arm'd thro' every street,
With poison'd darts, which not the good could shun,
   The speedy could out-fly, or valiant meet.

CCLXVIII

"The living few, and frequent funerals then,
   Proclaim'd thy wrath on this forsaken place;
And now those few who are return'd again,
   Thy searching judgments to their dwellings trace.

CCLXIX

"O pass not, Lord, an absolute decree,
   Or bind thy sentence unconditional;
But in thy sentence our remorse foresee,
   And, in that foresight, this thy doom recall.

CCLXX

"Thy threatings, Lord, as thine thou mayst revoke;
   But, if immutable and fix'd they stand,
Continue still thyself to give the stroke,
   And let not foreign foes oppress thy land."

CCLXXI

Th' Eternal heard, and from the heav'nly choir
   Chose out the cherub with the flaming sword;

And bade him swiftly drive th' approaching fire
   From where our naval magazins were stor'd.

CCLXXII

The blessed minister his wings display'd,
   And like a shooting star he cleft the night;
He charg'd the flames, and those that disobey'd
   He lash'd to duty with his sword of light.

CCLXXIII

The fugitive flames, chastis'd, went forth to prey
   On pious structures, by our fathers rear'd;
By which to heav'n they did affect the way,
   Ere faith in churchmen without works was heard.

CCLXXIV

The wanting orphans saw with wat'ry eyes
   Their founders' charity in dust laid low;
And sent to God their ever-answer'd cries,
   (For he protects the poor, who made them so.)

CCLXXV

Nor could thy fabric, Paul's, defend thee long,
   Tho' thou wert sacred to thy Maker's praise;
Tho' made immortal by a poet's song,
   And poets' songs the Theban walls could raise.

CCLXXVI

The daring flames peep'd in, and saw from far
   The awful beauties of the sacred choir;
But, since it was profan'd by civil war,
   Heav'n thought it fit to have it purg'd by fire.

CCLXXVII

Now down the narrow streets it swiftly came,
   And, widely opening, did on both sides prey:
This benefit we sadly owe the flame,
   If only ruin must enlarge our way.

CCLXXVIII

And now four days the sun had seen our woes;
　　Four nights the moon beheld th' incessant fire:
It seem'd as if the stars more sickly rose,
　　And farther from the fev'rish north retire.

CCLXXIX

In th' empyrean heaven, (the blest abode,)
　　The Thrones and the Dominions prostrate lie,
Not daring to behold their angry God;
　　And an hush'd silence damps the tuneful sky.

CCLXXX

At length th' Almighty cast a pitying eye,
　　And mercy softly touch'd his melting breast:
He saw the town's one half in rubbish lie,
　　And eager flames drive on to storm the rest.

CCLXXXI

An hollow crystal pyramid he takes,
　　In firmamental waters dipp'd above;
Of it a broad extinguisher he makes
　　And hoods the flames that to their quarry strove.

CCLXXXII

The vanquish'd fires withdraw from every place,
　　Or, full with feeding, sink into a sleep:
Each household genius shews again his face,
　　And from the hearths the little Lares creep.

CCLXXXIII

Our king this more than natural change beholds;
　　With sober joy his heart and eyes abound:
To the All-good his lifted hands he folds,
　　And thanks him low on his redeemed ground.

CCLXXXIV

As when sharp frosts had long constrain'd the earth,
　　A kindly thaw unlocks it with mild rain;

And first the tender blade peeps up to birth,
    And straight the green fields laugh with promis'd grain:

CCLXXXV

By such degrees the spreading gladness grew
    In every heart which fear had froze before;
The standing streets with so much joy they view,
    That with less grief the perish'd they deplore.

CCLXXXVI

The father of the people open'd wide
    His stores, and all the poor with plenty fed:
Thus God's anointed God's own place supplied,
    And fill'd the empty with his daily bread.

CCLXXXVII

This royal bounty brought its own reward,
    And in their minds so deep did print the sense,
That if their ruins sadly they regard,
    'T is but with fear the sight might drive him thence.

City's Request to the King Not to Leave Them

CCLXXXVIII

But so may he live long, that town to sway,
    Which by his auspice they will nobler make,
As he will hatch their ashes by his stay,
    And not their humble ruins now forsake.

CCLXXXIX

They have not lost their loyalty by fire;
    Nor is their courage or their wealth so low,
That from his wars they poorly would retire,
    Or beg the pity of a vanquish'd foe.

CCXC

Not with more constancy the Jews of old,
    By Cyrus from rewarded exile sent,
Their royal city did in dust behold,
    Or with more vigor to rebuild it went.

CCXCI

The utmost malice of their stars is past,
  And two dire comets, which have scourg'd the town,
In their own plague and fire have breath'd their last,
  Or, dimly, in their sinking sockets frown.

CCXCII

Now frequent trines the happier lights among,
  And high-rais'd Jove, from his dark prison freed,
(Those weights took off that on his planet hung,)
  Will gloriously the new-laid works succeed.

CCXCIII

Methinks already, from this chymic flame,
  I see a city of more precious mold,
Rich as the town which gives the Indies[b] name,
  With silver pav'd, and all divine with gold.

CCXCIV

Already, laboring with a mighty fate,
  She shakes the rubbish from her mounting brow,
And seems to have renew'd her charter's date,
  Which Heav'n will to the death of time allow.

CCXCV

More great than human, now, and more august,[c]
  New-deified she from her fires does rise:
Her widening streets on new foundations trust,
  And, opening, into larger parts she flies.

CCXCVI

Before, she like some shepherdess did show,
  Who sate to bathe her by a river's side;
Not answering to her fame, but rude and low,
  Nor taught the beauteous arts of modern pride.

---

[b]Mexico.
[c]*Augusta*, the old name of London.

CCXCVII

Now, like a maiden queen, she will behold,
  From her high turrets, hourly suitors come:
The East with incense, and the West with gold,
  Will stand, like suppliants, to receive her doom.

CCXCVIII

The silver Thames, her own domestic flood,
  Shall bear her vessels like a sweeping train;
And often wind, (as of his mistress proud,)
  With longing eyes to meet her face again.

CCXCIX

The wealthy Tagus, and the wealthier Rhine,
  The glory of their towns no more shall boast;
And Seine, that would with Belgian rivers join,
  Shall find her luster stain'd, and traffic lost.

CCC

The vent'rous merchant, who design'd more far,
  And touches on our hospitable shore,
Charm'd with the splendor of this northern star,
  Shall here unlade him, and depart no more.

CCCI

Our pow'rful navy shall no longer meet,
  The wealth of France or Holland to invade;
The beauty of this town, without a fleet,
  From all the world shall vindicate her trade.

CCCII

And, while this fam'd emporium we prepare,
  The British ocean shall such triumphs boast,
That those who now disdain our trade to share,
  Shall rob like pirates on our wealthy coast.

CCCIII

Already we have conquer'd half the war,
  And the less dang'rous part is left behind;

Our trouble now is but to make them dare,
   And not so great to vanquish as to find.

CCCIV

Thus to the eastern wealth thro' storms we go,
   But now, the Cape once doubled, fear no more;
A constant trade-wind will securely blow,
   And gently lay us on the spicy shore.

SONGS FROM *MARRIAGE À LA MODE*

[The date of this lively comedy, by Dryden, is fixed by the opening lines
of the prologue, which apparently "allude to the equipment of the fleet
which afterwards engaged the Dutch off Southwold Bay, May 28, 1672."
. . . The play was printed in 1673. . . . [B]oth songs appear also in *New
Court Songs and Poems, by R. V., Gent.*, 1672; and the second of them
in *Westminster Drollery, the Second Part*, 1672.]

I

I

Why should a foolish marriage vow,
   Which long ago was made,
Oblige us to each other now,
   When passion is decay'd?
We lov'd, and we lov'd, as long as we could,
   Till our love was lov'd out in us both;
But our marriage is dead, when the pleasure is fled:
   'T was pleasure first made it an oath.

II

If I have pleasures for a friend,
   And farther love in store,
What wrong has he whose joys did end,
   And who could give no more?
'T is a madness that he should be jealous of me,
   Or that I should bar him of another:
For all we can gain is to give ourselves pain,
   When neither can hinder the other.

II

I

Whilst Alexis lay press'd
  In her arms he lov'd best,
With his hands round her neck, and his head on her breast,
He found the fierce pleasure too hasty to stay,
And his soul in the tempest just flying away.

II

When Celia saw this,
  With a sigh and a kiss,
She cried: "O my dear, I am robb'd of my bliss!
'T is unkind to your love, and unfaithfully done,
To leave me behind you, and die all alone."

III

The youth, tho' in haste,
  And breathing his last,
In pity died slowly, while she died more fast;
Till at length she cried: "Now, my dear, now let us go;
Now die, my Alexis, and I will die too!"

IV

Thus intranc'd they did lie,
  Till Alexis did try
To recover new breath, that again he might die:
Then often they died; but the more they did so,
The nymph died more quick, and the shepherd more slow.

ABSALOM AND ACHITOPHEL

A POEM

Si propius stes
Te capiet magis.

[According to a note by Jacob Tonson,* "in the year 1680 Mr.
Dryden undertook the poem of *Absalom and Achitophel*, upon the
desire of King Charles the Second." . . . The poem was printed as a
folio pamphlet in 1681 . . . [and] was evidently meant to appear at
the psychological moment for exciting public sentiment against
Shaftesbury,† who was brought before the grand jury, on a charge of
high treason, on November 24. This first edition was anonymous;
and, though the authorship of the satire at once became known,
and was acknowledged by Dryden in his *Discourse concerning
Satire*, 1692 . . . , Dryden's name was never directly joined to it dur-
ing his lifetime. . . . Dryden seems to have taken the general idea of
applying to contemporary politics the scriptural story of the revolt of
Absalom (2 Samuel xiii–xviii), from an anonymous tract, published
in 1680, *Absalom's Conspiracy, or The Tragedy of Treason.*]

> In pious times, ere priestcraft did begin,
> Before polygamy was made a sin;
> When man on many multiplied his kind,
> Ere one to one was cursedly confin'd;
> When nature prompted, and no law denied
> Promiscuous use of concubine and bride;
> Then Israel's monarch after Heaven's own heart,
> His vigorous warmth did variously impart
> To wives and slaves; and, wide as his command,
> Scatter'd his Maker's image thro' the land.
> Michal, of royal blood, the crown did wear;
> A soil ungrateful to the tiller's care:
> Not so the rest; for several mothers bore

---

*[Jacob Tonson (c. 1656–1736) was the English publisher of Milton's *Paradise Lost*, as
well as works by John Dryden and Alexander Pope, among others.—ED.]
†In 1678 England had been thrown into a ferment by the "Popish Plot." During the next
three years party strife became so intense that the country seemed on the verge of civil
war. On the one side stood the Whigs, led by the Earl of Shaftesbury, who, using
Catholic intrigues, real and pretended, as his pretext, sought to exclude the Catholic
Duke of York from the throne in favor of the Duke of Monmouth. On the other side
stood the Tories, led in reality by the king himself, who, aided by secret grants of money
from France, strove to secure the succession for his brother, and indirectly did all in his
power to favor the Catholic cause. (From Part III of Mr. Noyes' "Biographical Sketch.")

To godlike David several sons before.
But since like slaves his bed they did ascend,
No true succession could their seed attend.
Of all this numerous progeny was none
So beautiful, so brave, as Absalon:
Whether, inspir'd by some diviner lust,
His father got him with a greater gust;
Or that his conscious destiny made way,
By manly beauty, to imperial sway.
Early in foreign fields he won renown,
With kings and states allied to Israel's crown:
In peace the thoughts of war he could remove,
And seem'd as he were only born for love.
Whate'er he did, was done with so much ease,
In him alone 't was natural to please:
His motions all accompanied with grace;
And paradise was open'd in his face.
With secret joy indulgent David view'd
His youthful image in his son renew'd:
To all his wishes nothing he denied;
And made the charming Annabel his bride.
What faults he had, (for who from faults is free?)
His father could not, or he would not see.
Some warm excesses which the law forbore,
Were construed youth that purg'd by boiling o'er,
And Amnon's murther, by a specious name,
Was call'd a just revenge for injur'd fame.
Thus prais'd and lov'd the noble youth remain'd,
While David, undisturb'd, in Sion reign'd.
But life can never be sincerely blest;
Heav'n punishes the bad, and proves the best.
The Jews, a headstrong, moody, murm'ring race,
As ever tried th' extent and stretch of grace;
God's pamper'd people, whom, debauch'd with ease,
No king could govern, nor no God could please;
(Gods they had tried of every shape and size,
That god-smiths could produce, or priests devise:)
These Adam-wits, too fortunately free,
Began to dream they wanted liberty;
And when no rule, no precedent was found,
Of men by laws less circumscrib'd and bound;
They led their wild desires to woods and caves,
And thought that all but savages were slaves.

They who, when Saul was dead, without a blow,
Made foolish Ishbosheth the crown forego;
Who banish'd David did from Hebron bring,
And with a general shout proclaim'd him king:
Those very Jews, who, at their very best,
Their humor more than loyalty express'd,
Now wonder'd why so long they had obey'd
An idol monarch, which their hands had made;
Thought they might ruin him they could create,
Or melt him to that golden calf, a State.
But these were random bolts; no form'd design,
Nor interest made the factious crowd to join:
The sober part of Israel, free from stain,
Well knew the value of a peaceful reign;
And, looking backward with a wise affright,
Saw seams of wounds, dishonest to the sight:
In contemplation of whose ugly scars
They curs'd the memory of civil wars.
The moderate sort of men, thus qualified,
Inclin'd the balance to the better side;
And David's mildness manag'd it so well,
The bad found no occasion to rebel.
But when to sin our bias'd nature leans,
The careful Devil is still at hand with means;
And providently pimps for ill desires:
The Good Old Cause reviv'd, a plot requires.
Plots, true or false, are necessary things,
To raise up commonwealths, and ruin kings.
    Th' inhabitants of old Jerusalem
Were Jebusites; the town so call'd from them;
And theirs the native right——
But when the chosen people grew more strong,
The rightful cause at length became the wrong;
And every loss the men of Jebus bore,
They still were thought God's enemies the more.
Thus worn and weaken'd, well or ill content,
Submit they must to David's government:
Impoverish'd and depriv'd of all command,
Their taxes doubled as they lost their land;
And, what was harder yet to flesh and blood,
Their gods disgrac'd, and burnt like common wood.
This set the heathen priesthood in a flame;
For priests of all religions are the same:

Of whatsoe'er descent their godhead be,
Stock, stone, or other homely pedigree,
In his defense his servants are as bold,
As if he had been born of beaten gold.
The Jewish rabbins, tho' their enemies,
In this conclude them honest men and wise:
For 't was their duty, all the learned think,
T' espouse his cause, by whom they eat and drink.
From hence began that Plot, the nation's curse,
Bad in itself, but represented worse;
Rais'd in extremes, and in extremes decried;
With oaths affirm'd, with dying vows denied;
Not weigh'd or winnow'd by the multitude;
But swallow'd in the mass, unchew'd and crude.
Some truth there was, but dash'd and brew'd with lies,
To please the fools, and puzzle all the wise.
Succeeding times did equal folly call,
Believing nothing, or believing all.
Th' Egyptian rites the Jebusites embrac'd;
Where gods were recommended by their taste.
Such sav'ry deities must needs be good,
As serv'd at once for worship and for food.
By force they could not introduce these gods,
For ten to one in former days was odds;
So fraud was us'd (the sacrificer's trade):
Fools are more hard to conquer than persuade.
Their busy teachers mingled with the Jews,
And rak'd for converts even the court and stews:
Which Hebrew priests the more unkindly took,
Because the fleece accompanies the flock.
Some thought they God's anointed meant to slay
By guns, invented since full many a day:
Our author swears it not; but who can know
How far the Devil and Jebusites may go?
This Plot, which fail'd for want of common sense,
Had yet a deep and dangerous consequence:
For, as when raging fevers boil the blood,
The standing lake soon floats into a flood,
And ev'ry hostile humor, which before
Slept quiet in its channels, bubbles o'er;
So several factions from this first ferment
Work up to foam, and threat the government.
Some by their friends, more by themselves thought wise,

Oppos'd the pow'r to which they could not rise.
Some had in courts been great, and thrown from thence,
Like fiends were harden'd in impenitence.
Some, by their monarch's fatal mercy, grown
From pardon'd rebels kinsmen to the throne,
Were rais'd in pow'r and public office high;
Strong bands, if bands ungrateful men could tie.
  Of these the false Achitophel was first;
A name to all succeeding ages curst:
For close designs, and crooked counsels fit;
Sagacious, bold, and turbulent of wit;
Restless, unfix'd in principles and place;
In pow'r unpleas'd, impatient of disgrace:
A fiery soul, which, working out its way,
Fretted the pigmy body to decay,
And o'er-inform'd the tenement of clay.
A daring pilot in extremity;
Pleas'd with the danger, when the waves went high,
He sought the storms; but, for a calm unfit,
Would steer too nigh the sands, to boast his wit.
Great wits are sure to madness near allied,
And thin partitions do their bounds divide;
Else why should he, with wealth and honor blest,
Refuse his age the needful hours of rest?
Punish a body which he could not please;
Bankrupt of life, yet prodigal of ease?
And all to leave what with his toil he won,
To that unfeather'd two-legg'd thing, a son;
Got, while his soul did huddled notions try;
And born a shapeless lump, like anarchy.
In friendship false, implacable in hate;
Resolv'd to ruin or to rule the State.
To compass this the triple bond he broke;
The pillars of the public safety shook;
And fitted Israel for a foreign yoke:
Then seiz'd with fear, yet still affecting fame,
Usurp'd a patriot's all-atoning name.
So easy still it proves in factious times,
With public zeal to cancel private crimes.
How safe is treason, and how sacred ill,
Where none can sin against the people's will!
Where crowds can wink, and no offense be known,
Since in another's guilt they find their own!

Yet fame deserv'd no enemy can grudge;
The statesman we abhor, but praise the judge.
In Israel's courts ne'er sat an Abbethdin
With more discerning eyes, or hands more clean;
Unbrib'd, unsought, the wretched to redress;
Swift of dispatch, and easy of access.
O, had he been content to serve the crown,
With virtues only proper to the gown;
Or had the rankness of the soil been freed
From cockle, that oppress'd the noble seed;
David for him his tuneful harp had strung,
And Heav'n had wanted one immortal song.
But wild Ambition loves to slide, not stand,
And Fortune's ice prefers to Virtue's land.
Achitophel, grown weary to possess
A lawful fame, and lazy happiness,
Disdain'd the golden fruit to gather free,
And lent the crowd his arm to shake the tree.
Now, manifest of crimes contriv'd long since,
He stood at bold defiance with his prince;
Held up the buckler of the people's cause
Against the crown, and skulk'd behind the laws.
The wish'd occasion of the Plot he takes;
Some circumstances finds, but more he makes.
By buzzing emissaries fills the ears
Of list'ning crowds with jealousies and fears
Of arbitrary counsels brought to light,
And proves the king himself a Jebusite.
Weak arguments! which yet he knew full well
Were strong with people easy to rebel.
For, govern'd by the moon, the giddy Jews
Tread the same track when she the prime renews;
And once in twenty years, their scribes record,
By natural instinct they change their lord.
Achitophel still wants a chief, and none
Was found so fit as warlike Absalon:
Not that he wish'd his greatness to create,
(For politicians neither love nor hate,)
But, for he knew his title not allow'd,
Would keep him still depending on the crowd:
That kingly pow'r, thus ebbing out, might be
Drawn to the dregs of a democracy.
Him he attempts with studied arts to please,

And sheds his venom in such words as these:
   "Auspicious prince, at whose nativity
Some royal planet rul'd the southern sky;
Thy longing country's darling and desire;
Their cloudy pillar and their guardian fire:
Their second Moses, whose extended wand
Divides the seas, and shews the promis'd land;
Whose dawning day in every distant age
Has exercis'd the sacred prophets' rage:
The people's pray'r, the glad diviners' theme,
The young men's vision, and the old men's dream!
Thee, Savior, thee, the nation's vows confess,
And, never satisfied with seeing, bless:
Swift unbespoken pomps thy steps proclaim,
And stammering babes are taught to lisp thy name.
How long wilt thou the general joy detain,
Starve and defraud the people of thy reign?
Content ingloriously to pass thy days
Like one of Virtue's fools that feeds on praise;
Till thy fresh glories, which now shine so bright,
Grow stale and tarnish with our daily sight.
Believe me, royal youth, thy fruit must be
Or gather'd ripe, or rot upon the tree.
Heav'n has to all allotted, soon or late,
Some lucky revolution of their fate;
Whose motions if we watch and guide with skill,
(For human good depends on human will,)
Our Fortune rolls as from a smooth descent,
And from the first impression takes the bent:
But, if unseiz'd, she glides away like wind,
And leaves repenting Folly far behind.
Now, now she meets you with a glorious prize,
And spreads her locks before her as she flies.
Had thus old David, from whose loins you spring,
Not dar'd, when Fortune call'd him, to be king,
At Gath an exile he might still remain,
And Heaven's anointing oil had been in vain.
Let his successful youth your hopes engage;
But shun th' example of declining age:
Behold him setting in his western skies,
The shadows lengthening as the vapors rise.
He is not now, as when on Jordan's sand
The joyful people throng'd to see him land,

Cov'ring the beach, and black'ning all the strand;
But, like the Prince of Angels, from his height
Comes tumbling downward with diminish'd light;
Betray'd by one poor plot to public scorn,
(Our only blessing since his curst return;)
Those heaps of people which one sheaf did bind,
Blown off and scatter'd by a puff of wind.
What strength can he to your designs oppose,
Naked of friends, and round beset with foes?
If Pharaoh's doubtful succor he should use,
A foreign aid would more incense the Jews:
Proud Egypt would dissembled friendship bring;
Foment the war, but not support the king:
Nor would the royal party e'er unite
With Pharaoh's arms t' assist the Jebusite;
Or if they should, their interest soon would break,
And with such odious aid make David weak.
All sorts of men by my successful arts,
Abhorring kings, estrange their alter'd hearts
From David's rule: and 't is the general cry,
'Religion, commonwealth, and liberty.'
If you, as champion of the public good,
Add to their arms a chief of royal blood,
What may not Israel hope, and what applause
Might such a general gain by such a cause?
Not barren praise alone, that gaudy flow'r
Fair only to the sight, but solid pow'r;
And nobler is a limited command,
Giv'n by the love of all your native land,
Than a successive title, long and dark,
Drawn from the moldy rolls of Noah's ark."
    What cannot praise effect in mighty minds,
When flattery soothes, and when ambition blinds!
Desire of pow'r, on earth a vicious weed,
Yet, sprung from high, is of celestial seed:
In God 't is glory; and when men aspire,
'T is but a spark too much of heavenly fire.
Th' ambitious youth, too covetous of fame,
Too full of angels' metal in his frame,
Unwarily was led from virtue's ways,
Made drunk with honor, and debauch'd with praise.
Half loth, and half consenting to the ill,
(For loyal blood within him struggled still,)

He thus replied: "And what pretense have I
To take up arms for public liberty?
My father governs with unquestion'd right;
The faith's defender, and mankind's delight;
Good, gracious, just, observant of the laws:
And Heav'n by wonders has espous'd his cause.
Whom has he wrong'd in all his peaceful reign?
Who sues for justice to his throne in vain?
What millions has he pardon'd of his foes,
Whom just revenge did to his wrath expose?
Mild, easy, humble, studious of our good;
Enclin'd to mercy, and averse from blood;
If mildness ill with stubborn Israel suit,
His crime is God's beloved attribute.
What could he gain, his people to betray,
Or change his right for arbitrary sway?
Let haughty Pharaoh curse with such a reign
His fruitful Nile, and yoke a servile train.
If David's rule Jerusalem displease,
The Dog-star heats their brains to this disease.
Why then should I, encouraging the bad,
Turn rebel and run popularly mad?
Were he a tyrant, who, by lawless might
Oppress'd the Jews, and rais'd the Jebusite,
Well might I mourn; but nature's holy bands
Would curb my spirits and restrain my hands:
The people might assert their liberty;
But what was right in them were crime in me.
His favor leaves me nothing to require,
Prevents my wishes, and outruns desire.
What more can I expect while David lives?
All but his kingly diadem he gives:
And that"—But there he paus'd; then sighing, said—
"Is justly destin'd for a worthier head.
For when my father from his toils shall rest,
And late augment the number of the blest,
His lawful issue shall the throne ascend,
Or the collat'ral line, where that shall end.
His brother, tho' oppress'd with vulgar spite,
Yet dauntless, and secure of native right,
Of every royal virtue stands possess'd;
Still dear to all the bravest and the best.
His courage foes, his friends his truth proclaim;

His loyalty the king, the world his fame.
His mercy ev'n th' offending crowd will find;
For sure he comes of a forgiving kind.
Why should I then repine at Heaven's decree,
Which gives me no pretense to royalty?
Yet O that fate, propitiously inclin'd,
Had rais'd my birth, or had debas'd my mind;
To my large soul not all her treasure lent,
And then betray'd it to a mean descent!
I find, I find my mounting spirits bold,
And David's part disdains my mother's mold.
Why am I scanted by a niggard birth?
My soul disclaims the kindred of her earth;
And, made for empire, whispers me within,
'Desire of greatness is a godlike sin.'"
　　Him staggering so when hell's dire agent found,
While fainting Virtue scarce maintain'd her ground,
He pours fresh forces in, and thus replies:
　　"Th' eternal God, supremely good and wise,
Imparts not these prodigious gifts in vain:
What wonders are reserv'd to bless your reign!
Against your will, your arguments have shown,
Such virtue 's only giv'n to guide a throne.
Not that your father's mildness I contemn;
But manly force becomes the diadem.
'T is true he grants the people all they crave;
And more, perhaps, than subjects ought to have:
For lavish grants suppose a monarch tame,
And more his goodness than his wit proclaim.
But when should people strive their bonds to break,
If not when kings are negligent or weak?
Let him give on till he can give no more,
The thrifty Sanhedrin shall keep him poor;
And every shekel which he can receive,
Shall cost a limb of his prerogative.
To ply him with new plots shall be my care;
Or plunge him deep in some expensive war;
Which when his treasure can no more supply,
He must, with the remains of kingship, buy.
His faithful friends, our jealousies and fears
Call Jebusites, and Pharaoh's pensioners;
Whom when our fury from his aid has torn,
He shall be naked left to public scorn.

The next successor, whom I fear and hate,
My arts have made obnoxious to the State;
Turn'd all his virtues to his overthrow,
And gain'd our elders to pronounce a foe.
His right, for sums of necessary gold,
Shall first be pawn'd, and afterwards be sold;
Till time shall ever-wanting David draw,
To pass your doubtful title into law:
If not, the people have a right supreme
To make their kings; for kings are made for them.
All empire is no more than pow'r in trust,
Which, when resum'd, can be no longer just.
Succession, for the general good design'd,
In its own wrong a nation cannot bind;
If altering that the people can relieve,
Better one suffer than a nation grieve.
The Jews well know their pow'r: ere Saul they chose,
God was their king, and God they durst depose.
Urge now your piety, your filial name,
A father's right, and fear of future fame;
The public good, that universal call,
To which even Heav'n submitted, answers all.
Nor let his love enchant your generous mind;
'T is Nature's trick to propagate her kind.
Our fond begetters, who would never die,
Love but themselves in their posterity.
Or let his kindness by th' effects be tried,
Or let him lay his vain pretense aside.
God said he lov'd your father; could he bring
A better proof, than to anoint him king?
It surely shew'd he lov'd the shepherd well,
Who gave so fair a flock as Israel.
Would David have you thought his darling son?
What means he then, to alienate the crown?
The name of godly he may blush to bear:
'T is after God's own heart to cheat his heir.
He to his brother gives supreme command,
To you a legacy of barren land:
Perhaps th' old harp, on which he thrums his lays,
Or some dull Hebrew ballad in your praise.
Then the next heir, a prince severe and wise,
Already looks on you with jealous eyes;
Sees thro' the thin disguises of your arts,

And marks your progress in the people's hearts.
Tho' now his mighty soul its grief contains,
He meditates revenge who least complains;
And, like a lion, slumb'ring in the way,
Or sleep dissembling, while he waits his prey,
His fearless foes within his distance draws,
Constrains his roaring, and contracts his paws;
Till at the last, his time for fury found,
He shoots with sudden vengeance from the ground;
The prostrate vulgar passes o'er and spares,
But with a lordly rage his hunters tears.
Your case no tame expedients will afford:
Resolve on death, or conquest by the sword,
Which for no less a stake than life you draw;
And self-defense is nature's eldest law.
Leave the warm people no considering time;
For then rebellion may be thought a crime.
Prevail yourself of what occasion gives,
But try your title while your father lives;
And that your arms may have a fair pretense,
Proclaim you take them in the king's defense;
Whose sacred life each minute would expose
To plots, from seeming friends, and secret foes.
And who can sound the depth of David's soul?
Perhaps his fear his kindness may control.
He fears his brother, tho' he loves his son,
For plighted vows too late to be undone.
If so, by force he wishes to be gain'd;
Like women's lechery, to seem constrain'd.
Doubt not: but, when he most affects the frown,
Commit a pleasing rape upon the crown.
Secure his person to secure your cause:
They who possess the prince, possess the laws."
    He said, and this advice above the rest,
With Absalom's mild nature suited best:
Unblam'd of life, (ambition set aside,)
Not stain'd with cruelty, nor puff'd with pride;
How happy had he been, if destiny
Had higher plac'd his birth, or not so high!
His kingly virtues might have claim'd a throne,
And blest all other countries but his own.
But charming greatness since so few refuse,
'T is juster to lament him than accuse.

Strong were his hopes a rival to remove,
With blandishments to gain the public love;
To head the faction while their zeal was hot,
And popularly prosecute the Plot.
To farther this, Achitophel unites
The malcontents of all the Israelites;
Whose differing parties he could wisely join,
For several ends, to serve the same design:
The best, (and of the princes some were such,)
Who thought the pow'r of monarchy too much;
Mistaken men, and patriots in their hearts;
Not wicked, but seduc'd by impious arts.
By these the springs of property were bent,
And wound so high, they crack'd the government.
The next for interest sought t' embroil the State,
To sell their duty at a dearer rate;
And make their Jewish markets of the throne,
Pretending public good, to serve their own.
Others thought kings an useless heavy load,
Who cost too much, and did too little good.
These were for laying honest David by,
On principles of pure good husbandry.
With them join'd all th' haranguers of the throng,
That thought to get preferment by the tongue.
Who follow next, a double danger bring,
Not only hating David, but the king:
The Solymæan rout, well-vers'd of old
In godly faction, and in treason bold;
Cow'ring and quaking at a conqu'ror's sword;
But lofty to a lawful prince restor'd;
Saw with disdain an Ethnic plot begun,
And scorn'd by Jebusites to be outdone.
Hot Levites headed these; who, pull'd before
From th' ark, which in the Judges' days they bore,
Resum'd their cant, and with a zealous cry
Pursued their old belov'd Theocracy:
Where Sanhedrin and priest enslav'd the nation,
And justified their spoils by inspiration:
For who so fit for reign as Aaron's race,
If once dominion they could found in grace?
These led the pack; tho' not of surest scent,
Yet deepest mouth'd against the government.
A numerous host of dreaming saints succeed,

Of the true old enthusiastic breed:
'Gainst form and order they their pow'r imploy,
Nothing to build, and all things to destroy.
But far more numerous was the herd of such,
Who think too little, and who talk too much.
These, out of mere instinct, they knew not why,
Ador'd their fathers' God and property;
And, by the same blind benefit of fate,
The Devil and the Jebusite did hate:
Born to be sav'd, even in their own despite,
Because they could not help believing right.
Such were the tools; but a whole Hydra more
Remains, of sprouting heads too long to score.
Some of their chiefs were princes of the land:
In the first rank of these did Zimri stand;
A man so various, that he seem'd to be
Not one, but all mankind's epitome:
Stiff in opinions, always in the wrong;
Was everything by starts, and nothing long;
But, in the course of one revolving moon,
Was chymist, fiddler, statesman, and buffoon:
Then all for women, painting, rhyming, drinking,
Besides ten thousand freaks that died in thinking.
Blest madman, who could every hour employ,
With something new to wish, or to enjoy!
Railing and praising were his usual themes;
And both (to shew his judgment) in extremes:
So over-violent, or over-civil,
That every man, with him, was God or Devil.
In squand'ring wealth was his peculiar art:
Nothing went unrewarded but desert.
Beggar'd by fools, whom still he found too late,
He had his jest, and they had his estate.
He laugh'd himself from court; then sought relief
By forming parties, but could ne'er be chief;
For, spite of him, the weight of business fell
On Absalom and wise Achitophel:
Thus, wicked but in will, of means bereft,
He left not faction, but of that was left.
    Titles and names 't were tedious to rehearse
Of lords, below the dignity of verse.
Wits, warriors, Commonwealth's-men, were the best;
Kind husbands, and mere nobles, all the rest.

And therefore, in the name of dulness, be
The well-hung Balaam and cold Caleb, free;
And canting Nadab let oblivion damn,
Who made new porridge for the paschal lamb.
Let friendship's holy band some names assure;
Some their own worth, and some let scorn secure.
Nor shall the rascal rabble here have place,
Whom kings no titles gave, and God no grace:
Not bull-fac'd Jonas, who could statutes draw
To mean rebellion, and make treason law.
But he, tho' bad, is follow'd by a worse,
The wretch who Heav'n's anointed dar'd to curse:
Shimei, whose youth did early promise bring
Of zeal to God and hatred to his king,
Did wisely from expensive sins refrain,
And never broke the Sabbath, but for gain;
Nor ever was he known an oath to vent,
Or curse, unless against the government.
Thus heaping wealth, by the most ready way
Among the Jews, which was to cheat and pray,
The city, to reward his pious hate
Against his master, chose him magistrate.
His hand a vare of justice did uphold;
His neck was loaded with a chain of gold.
During his office, treason was no crime;
The sons of Belial had a glorious time;
For Shimei, tho' not prodigal of pelf,
Yet lov'd his wicked neighbor as himself.
When two or three were gather'd to declaim
Against the monarch of Jerusalem,
Shimei was always in the midst of them;
And if they curs'd the king when he was by,
Would rather curse than break good company.
If any durst his factious friends accuse,
He pack'd a jury of dissenting Jews;
Whose fellow-feeling in the godly cause
Would free the suff'ring saint from human laws.
For laws are only made to punish those
Who serve the king, and to protect his foes.
If any leisure time he had from pow'r,
(Because 't is sin to misimploy an hour,)
His bus'ness was, by writing, to persuade
That kings were useless, and a clog to trade;

And, that his noble style he might refine,
No Rechabite more shunn'd the fumes of wine.
Chaste were his cellars, and his shrieval board
The grossness of a city feast abhorr'd:
His cooks, with long disuse, their trade forgot;
Cool was his kitchen, tho' his brains were hot.
Such frugal virtue malice may accuse,
But sure 't was necessary to the Jews;
For towns once burnt such magistrates require
As dare not tempt God's providence by fire.
With spiritual food he fed his servants well,
But free from flesh that made the Jews rebel;
And Moses' laws he held in more account,
For forty days of fasting in the mount.
To speak the rest, who better are forgot,
Would tire a well-breath'd witness of the Plot.
Yet, Corah, thou shalt from oblivion pass:
Erect thyself, thou monumental brass,
High as the serpent of thy metal made,
While nations stand secure beneath thy shade.
What tho' his birth were base, yet comets rise
From earthy vapors, ere they shine in skies.
Prodigious actions may as well be done
By weaver's issue, as by prince's son.
This arch-attestor for the public good
By that one deed ennobles all his blood.
Who ever ask'd the witnesses' high race,
Whose oath with martyrdom did Stephen grace?
Ours was a Levite, and as times went then,
His tribe were God Almighty's gentlemen.
Sunk were his eyes, his voice was harsh and loud,
Sure signs he neither choleric was nor proud:
His long chin prov'd his wit; his saintlike grace
A church vermilion, and a Moses' face.
His memory, miraculously great,
Could plots, exceeding man's belief, repeat;
Which therefore cannot be accounted lies,
For human wit could never such devise.
Some future truths are mingled in his book;
But where the witness fail'd, the prophet spoke:
Some things like visionary flights appear;
The spirit caught him up, the Lord knows where;
And gave him his rabbinical degree,

Unknown to foreign university.
His judgment yet his mem'ry did excel;
Which piec'd his wondrous evidence so well,
And suited to the temper of the times,
Then groaning under Jebusitic crimes.
Let Israel's foes suspect his heav'nly call,
And rashly judge his writ apocryphal;
Our laws for such affronts have forfeits made:
He takes his life, who takes away his trade.
Were I myself in witness Corah's place,
The wretch who did me such a dire disgrace,
Should whet my memory, tho' once forgot,
To make him an appendix of my plot.
His zeal to Heav'n made him his prince despise,
And load his person with indignities;
But zeal peculiar privilege affords,
Indulging latitude to deeds and words;
And Corah might for Agag's murther call,
In terms as coarse as Samuel us'd to Saul.
What others in his evidence did join,
(The best that could be had for love or coin,)
In Corah's own predicament will fall;
For witness is a common name to all.
    Surrounded thus with friends of every sort,
Deluded Absalom forsakes the court;
Impatient of high hopes, urg'd with renown,
And fir'd with near possession of a crown.
Th' admiring crowd are dazzled with surprise,
And on his goodly person feed their eyes.
His joy conceal'd, he sets himself to show,
On each side bowing popularly low;
His looks, his gestures, and his words he frames,
And with familiar ease repeats their names.
Thus form'd by nature, furnish'd out with arts,
He glides unfelt into their secret hearts.
Then, with a kind compassionating look,
And sighs, bespeaking pity ere he spoke,
Few words he said; but easy those and fit,
More slow than Hybla-drops, and far more sweet.
    "I mourn, my countrymen, your lost estate;
Tho' far unable to prevent your fate:
Behold a banish'd man, for your dear cause
Expos'd a prey to arbitrary laws!

Yet O! that I alone could be undone,
Cut off from empire, and no more a son!
Now all your liberties a spoil are made;
Egypt and Tyrus intercept your trade,
And Jebusites your sacred rites invade.
My father, whom with reverence yet I name,
Charm'd into ease, is careless of his fame;
And, brib'd with petty sums of foreign gold,
Is grown in Bathsheba's embraces old;
Exalts his enemies, his friends destroys;
And all his pow'r against himself imploys.
He gives, and let him give, my right away;
But why should he his own and yours betray?
He, only he, can make the nation bleed,
And he alone from my revenge is freed.
Take then my tears, (with that he wip'd his eyes,)
'T is all the aid my present pow'r supplies:
No court-informer can these arms accuse;
These arms may sons against their fathers use:
And 't is my wish, the next successor's reign
May make no other Israelite complain."
   Youth, beauty, graceful action seldom fail;
But common interest always will prevail;
And pity never ceases to be shown
To him who makes the people's wrongs his own.
The crowd, that still believe their kings oppress,
With lifted hands their young Messiah bless:
Who now begins his progress to ordain
With chariots, horsemen, and a num'rous train;
From east to west his glories he displays,
And, like the sun, the promis'd land surveys.
Fame runs before him as the morning star,
And shouts of joy salute him from afar:
Each house receives him as a guardian god,
And consecrates the place of his abode.
But hospitable treats did most commend
Wise Issachar, his wealthy western friend.
This moving court, that caught the people's eyes,
And seem'd but pomp, did other ends disguise:
Achitophel had form'd it, with intent
To sound the depths, and fathom, where it went,
The people's hearts; distinguish friends from foes,
And try their strength, before they came to blows.

Yet all was color'd with a smooth pretense
Of specious love, and duty to their prince.
Religion, and redress of grievances,
Two names that always cheat and always please,
Are often urg'd; and good King David's life
Endanger'd by a brother and a wife.
Thus in a pageant shew a plot is made,
And peace itself is war in masquerade.
O foolish Israel! never warn'd by ill!
Still the same bait, and circumvented still!
Did ever men forsake their present ease,
In midst of health imagine a disease;
Take pains contingent mischiefs to foresee,
Make heirs for monarchs, and for God decree?
What shall we think! Can people give away,
Both for themselves and sons, their native sway?
Then they are left defenseless to the sword
Of each unbounded, arbitrary lord:
And laws are vain, by which we right enjoy,
If kings unquestion'd can those laws destroy.
Yet if the crowd be judge of fit and just,
And kings are only officers in trust,
Then this resuming cov'nant was declar'd
When kings were made, or is for ever barr'd.
If those who gave the scepter could not tie
By their own deed their own posterity,
How then could Adam bind his future race?
How could his forfeit on mankind take place?
Or how could heavenly justice damn us all,
Who ne'er consented to our father's fall?
Then kings are slaves to those whom they command,
And tenants to their people's pleasure stand.
Add, that the pow'r for property allow'd
Is mischievously seated in the crowd;
For who can be secure of private right,
If sovereign sway may be dissolv'd by might?
Nor is the people's judgment always true:
The most may err as grossly as the few;
And faultless kings run down, by common cry,
For vice, oppression, and for tyranny.
What standard is there in a fickle rout,
Which, flowing to the mark, runs faster out?
Now only crowds, but Sanhedrins may be

Infected with this public lunacy,
And share the madness of rebellious times,
To murther monarchs for imagin'd crimes.
If they may give and take whene'er they please,
Not kings alone, (the Godhead's images,)
But government itself at length must fall
To nature's state, where all have right to all.
Yet, grant our lords the people kings can make,
What prudent men a settled throne would shake?
For whatsoe'er their sufferings were before,
That change they covet makes them suffer more.
All other errors but disturb a state,
But innovation is the blow of fate.
If ancient fabrics nod, and threat to fall,
To patch the flaws, and buttress up the wall,
Thus far 't is duty: but here fix the mark;
For all beyond it is to touch our ark.
To change foundations, cast the frame anew,
Is work for rebels, who base ends pursue,
At once divine and human laws control,
And mend the parts by ruin of the whole.
The tamp'ring world is subject to this curse,
To physic their disease into a worse.
       Now what relief can righteous David bring?
How fatal 't is to be too good a king!
Friends he has few, so high the madness grows:
Who dare be such, must be the people's foes.
Yet some there were, ev'n in the worst of days;
Some let me name, and naming is to praise.
       In this short file Barzillai first appears;
Barzillai, crown'd with honor and with years.
Long since, the rising rebels he withstood
In regions waste, beyond the Jordan's flood:
Unfortunately brave to buoy the State;
But sinking underneath his master's fate:
In exile with his godlike prince he mourn'd;
For him he suffer'd, and with him return'd.
The court he practic'd, not the courtier's art:
Large was his wealth, but larger was his heart,
Which well the noblest objects knew to choose,
The fighting warrior, and recording Muse.
His bed could once a fruitful issue boast;
Now more than half a father's name is lost.

His eldest hope, with every grace adorn'd,
By me (so Heav'n will have it) always mourn'd,
And always honor'd, snatch'd in manhood's prime
B' unequal fates, and Providence's crime;
Yet not before the goal of honor won,
All parts fulfill'd of subject and of son:
Swift was the race, but short the time to run.
O narrow circle, but of pow'r divine,
Scanted in space, but perfect in thy line!
By sea, by land, thy matchless worth was known,
Arms thy delight, and war was all thy own:
Thy force, infus'd, the fainting Tyrians propp'd;
And haughty Pharaoh found his fortune stopp'd.
O ancient honor! O unconquer'd hand,
Whom foes unpunish'd never could withstand!
But Israel was unworthy of thy name;
Short is the date of all immoderate fame.
It looks as Heav'n our ruin had design'd,
And durst not trust thy fortune and thy mind.
Now, free from earth, thy disencumber'd soul
Mounts up, and leaves behind the clouds and starry pole:
From thence thy kindred legions mayst thou bring,
To aid the guardian angel of thy king.
Here stop, my Muse, here cease thy painful flight;
No pinions can pursue immortal height:
Tell good Barzillai thou canst sing no more,
And tell thy soul she should have fled before.
Or fled she with his life, and left this verse
To hang on her departed patron's hearse?
Now take thy steepy flight from heav'n, and see
If thou canst find on earth another he:
Another he would be too hard to find;
See then whom thou canst see not far behind.
Zadoc the priest, whom, shunning pow'r and place,
His lowly mind advanc'd to David's grace.
With him the Sagan of Jerusalem,
Of hospitable soul, and noble stem;
Him of the western dome, whose weighty sense
Flows in fit words and heavenly eloquence.
The prophets' sons, by such example led,
To learning and to loyalty were bred:
For colleges on bounteous kings depend,
And never rebel was to arts a friend.

To these succeed the pillars of the laws;
Who best could plead, and best can judge a cause.
Next them a train of loyal peers ascend;
Sharp-judging Adriel, the Muses' friend;
Himself a Muse—in Sanhedrin's debate
True to his prince, but not a slave of state:
Whom David's love with honors did adorn,
That from his disobedient son were torn.
Jotham of piercing wit, and pregnant thought;
Endued by nature, and by learning taught
To move assemblies, who but only tried
The worse a while, then chose the better side:
Nor chose alone, but turn'd the balance too;
So much the weight of one brave man can do.
Hushai, the friend of David in distress;
In public storms, of manly steadfastness:
By foreign treaties he inform'd his youth,
And join'd experience to his native truth.
His frugal care supplied the wanting throne;
Frugal for that, but bounteous of his own:
'T is easy conduct when exchequers flow,
But hard the task to manage well the low;
For sovereign power is too depress'd or high,
When kings are forc'd to sell, or crowds to buy.
Indulge one labor more, my weary Muse,
For Amiel: who can Amiel's praise refuse?
Of ancient race by birth, but nobler yet
In his own worth, and without title great:
The Sanhedrin long time as chief he rul'd,
Their reason guided, and their passion cool'd:
So dext'rous was he in the crown's defense,
So form'd to speak a loyal nation's sense,
That, as their band was Israel's tribes in small,
So fit was he to represent them all.
Now rasher charioteers the seat ascend,
Whose loose careers his steady skill commend:
They, like th' unequal ruler of the day,
Misguide the seasons, and mistake the way;
While he withdrawn at their mad labor smiles,
And safe enjoys the sabbath of his toils.
    These were the chief, a small but faithful band
Of worthies, in the breach who dar'd to stand,
And tempt th' united fury of the land.

With grief they view'd such powerful engines bent,
To batter down the lawful government:
A numerous faction, with pretended frights,
In Sanhedrins to plume the regal rights;
The true successor from the court remov'd;
The Plot, by hireling witnesses, improv'd.
These ills they saw, and, as their duty bound,
They shew'd the king the danger of the wound;
That no concessions from the throne would please,
But lenitives fomented the disease;
That Absalom, ambitious of the crown,
Was made the lure to draw the people down;
That false Achitophel's pernicious hate
Had turn'd the Plot to ruin Church and State;
The council violent, the rabble worse;
That Shimei taught Jerusalem to curse.
    With all these loads of injuries oppress'd,
And long revolving in his careful breast
Th' event of things, at last, his patience tir'd,
Thus from his royal throne, by Heav'n inspir'd,
The godlike David spoke: with awful fear
His train their Maker in their master hear.
    "Thus long have I, by native mercy sway'd,
My wrongs dissembled, my revenge delay'd:
So willing to forgive th' offending age;
So much the father did the king assuage.
But now so far my clemency they slight,
Th' offenders question my forgiving right.
That one was made for many, they contend;
But 't is to rule; for that 's a monarch's end.
They call my tenderness of blood, my fear;
Tho' manly tempers can the longest bear.
Yet, since they will divert my native course,
'T is time to shew I am not good by force.
Those heap'd affronts that haughty subjects bring,
Are burthens for a camel, not a king.
Kings are the public pillars of the State,
Born to sustain and prop the nation's weight;
If my young Samson will pretend a call
To shake the column, let him share the fall:
But O that yet he would repent and live!
How easy 't is for parents to forgive!
With how few tears a pardon might be won

From nature, pleading for a darling son!
Poor pitied youth, by my paternal care
Rais'd up to all the height his frame could bear!
Had God ordain'd his fate for empire born,
He would have giv'n his soul another turn:
Gull'd with a patriot's name, whose modern sense
Is one that would by law supplant his prince;
The people's brave, the politician's tool;
Never was patriot yet, but was a fool.
Whence comes it that religion and the laws
Should more be Absalom's than David's cause?
His old instructor, ere he lost his place,
Was never thought indued with so much grace.
Good heav'ns, how faction can a patriot paint!
My rebel ever proves my people's saint.
Would they impose an heir upon the throne?
Let Sanhedrins be taught to give their own.
A king 's at least a part of government,
And mine as requisite as their consent;
Without my leave a future king to choose,
Infers a right the present to depose.
True, they petition me t' approve their choice;
But Esau's hands suit ill with Jacob's voice.
My pious subjects for my safety pray;
Which to secure, they take my pow'r away.
From plots and treasons Heav'n preserve my years,
But save me most from my petitioners!
Unsatiate as the barren womb or grave;
God cannot grant so much as they can crave.
What then is left, but with a jealous eye
To guard the small remains of royalty?
The law shall still direct my peaceful sway,
And the same law teach rebels to obey:
Votes shall no more establish'd pow'r control—
Such votes as make a part exceed the whole:
No groundless clamors shall my friends remove,
Nor crowds have pow'r to punish ere they prove;
For gods and godlike kings their care express,
Still to defend their servants in distress.
O that my pow'r to saving were confin'd!
Why am I forc'd, like Heav'n, against my mind,
To make examples of another kind?
Must I at length the sword of justice draw?

O curst effects of necessary law!
How ill my fear they by my mercy scan!
Beware the fury of a patient man.
Law they require, let Law then shew her face;
They could not be content to look on Grace,
Her hinder parts, but with a daring eye
To tempt the terror of her front and die.
By their own arts, 't is righteously decreed,
Those dire artificers of death shall bleed.
Against themselves their witnesses will swear,
Till viper-like their mother Plot they tear;
And suck for nutriment that bloody gore,
Which was their principle of life before.
Their Belial with their Belzebub will fight;
Thus on my foes, my foes shall do me right.
Nor doubt th' event; for factious crowds engage,
In their first onset, all their brutal rage.
Then let 'em take an unresisted course;
Retire, and traverse, and delude their force;
But, when they stand all breathless, urge the fight,
And rise upon 'em with redoubled might;
For lawful pow'r is still superior found;
When long driv'n back, at length it stands the ground."
    He said. Th' Almighty, nodding, gave consent;
And peals of thunder shook the firmament.
Henceforth a series of new time began,
The mighty years in long procession ran:
Once more the godlike David was restor'd,
And willing nations knew their lawful lord.

MAC FLECKNOE

[Thomas Shadwell, once Dryden's friend . . . , now his enemy, and an ardent Whig, had published an answer to *The Medal*, entitled, *The Medal of John Bayes, a Satire against Folly and Knavery*, in which he assailed Dryden with foul and scurrilous abuse. Dryden's reply was the following poem, published . . . on October 4, 1682. . . . A second edition, with numerous changes in the text, appeared as the first piece in *Miscellany Poems*, 1684, from which the present text is taken.]

All human things are subject to decay,
And when fate summons, monarchs must obey.
This Flecknoe found, who, like Augustus, young
Was call'd to empire, and had govern'd long;
In prose and verse, was own'd, without dispute,
Thro' all the realms of Nonsense, absolute.
This aged prince, now flourishing in peace,
And blest with issue of a large increase;
Worn out with business, did at length debate
To settle the succession of the State;
And, pond'ring which of all his sons was fit
To reign, and wage immortal war with wit,
Cried: "'T is resolv'd; for nature pleads, that he
Should only rule, who most resembles me.
Sh—— alone my perfect image bears,
Mature in dulness from his tender years:
Sh—— alone, of all my sons, is he
Who stands confirm'd in full stupidity.
The rest to some faint meaning make pretense,
But Sh—— never deviates into sense.
Some beams of wit on other souls may fall,
Strike thro', and make a lucid interval;
But Sh——'s genuine night admits no ray,
His rising fogs prevail upon the day.
Besides, his goodly fabric fills the eye,
And seems design'd for thoughtless majesty;
Thoughtless as monarch oaks that shade the plain,
And, spread in solemn state, supinely reign.
Heywood and Shirley were but types of thee,
Thou last great prophet of tautology.
Even I, a dunce of more renown than they,
Was sent before but to prepare thy way;
And, coarsely clad in Norwich drugget, came

To teach the nations in thy greater name.
My warbling lute, the lute I whilom strung,
When to King John of Portugal I sung,
Was but the prelude to that glorious day,
When thou on silver Thames didst cut thy way,
With well-tim'd oars before the royal barge,
Swell'd with the pride of thy celestial charge;
And big with hymn, commander of a host,
The like was ne'er in Epsom blankets toss'd.
Methinks I see the new Arion sail,
The lute still trembling underneath thy nail.
At thy well-sharpen'd thumb from shore to shore
The treble squeaks for fear, the basses roar;
Echoes from Pissing Alley Sh—— call,
And Sh—— they resound from Aston Hall.
About thy boat the little fishes throng,
As at the morning toast that floats along.
Sometimes, as prince of thy harmonious band,
Thou wield'st thy papers in thy threshing hand.
St. André's feet ne'er kept more equal time,
Not ev'n the feet of thy own Psyche's rhyme;
Tho' they in number as in sense excel:
So just, so like tautology, they fell,
That, pale with envy, Singleton forswore
The lute and sword, which he in triumph bore,
And vow'd he ne'er would act Villerius more."
Here stopp'd the good old sire, and wept for joy
In silent raptures of the hopeful boy.
All arguments, but most his plays, persuade,
That for anointed dulness he was made.

    Close to the walls which fair Augusta bind,
(The fair Augusta much to fears inclin'd,)
An ancient fabric rais'd t' inform the sight,
There stood of yore, and Barbican it hight:
A watchtower once; but now, so fate ordains,
Of all the pile an empty name remains.
From its old ruins brothel-houses rise,
Scenes of lewd loves, and of polluted joys,
Where their vast courts the mother-strumpets keep,
And, undisturb'd by watch, in silence sleep.
Near these a Nursery erects its head,
Where queens are form'd, and future heroes bred;
Where unfledg'd actors learn to laugh and cry,

Where infant punks their tender voices try,
And little Maximins the gods defy.
Great Fletcher never treads in buskins here,
Nor greater Jonson dares in socks appear;
But gentle Simkin just reception finds
Amidst this monument of vanish'd minds:
Pure clinches the suburbian Muse affords,
And Panton waging harmless war with words.
Here Flecknoe, as a place to fame well known,
Ambitiously design'd his Sh——'s throne;
For ancient Dekker prophesied long since,
That in this pile should reign a mighty prince,
Born for a scourge of wit, and flail of sense;
To whom true dulness should some Psyches owe,
But worlds of Misers from his pen should flow;
Humorists and hypocrites it should produce,
Whole Raymond families, and tribes of Bruce.
    Now Empress Fame had publish'd the renown
Of Sh——'s coronation thro' the town.
Rous'd by report of Fame, the nations meet,
From near Bunhill, and distant Watling Street.
No Persian carpets spread th' imperial way,
But scatter'd limbs of mangled poets lay;
From dusty shops neglected authors come,
Martyrs of pies, and relics of the bum.
Much Heywood, Shirley, Ogleby there lay,
But loads of Sh—— almost chok'd the way.
Bilk'd stationers for yeomen stood prepar'd,
And Herringman was captain of the guard.
The hoary prince in majesty appear'd,
High on a throne of his own labors rear'd.
At his right hand our young Ascanius sate,
Rome's other hope, and pillar of the State.
His brows thick fogs, instead of glories, grace,
And lambent dulness play'd around his face.
As Hannibal did to the altars come,
Sworn by his sire a mortal foe to Rome;
So Sh—— swore, nor should his vow be vain,
That he till death true dulness would maintain;
And, in his father's right, and realm's defense,
Ne'er to have peace with wit, nor truce with sense.
The king himself the sacred unction made,
As king by office, and as priest by trade.

In his sinister hand, instead of ball,
He plac'd a mighty mug of potent ale;
Love's Kingdom to his right he did convey,
At once his scepter, and his rule of sway;
Whose righteous lore the prince had practic'd young,
And from whose loins recorded Psyche sprung.
His temples, last, with poppies were o'erspread,
That nodding seem'd to consecrate his head.
Just at that point of time, if fame not lie,
On his left hand twelve reverend owls did fly.
So Romulus, 't is sung, by Tiber's brook,
Presage of sway from twice six vultures took.
Th' admiring throng loud acclamations make,
And omens of his future empire take.
The sire then shook the honors of his head,
And from his brows damps of oblivion shed
Full on the filial dulness: long he stood,
Repelling from his breast the raging god;
At length burst out in this prophetic mood:
    "Heavens bless my son, from Ireland let him reign
To far Barbadoes on the western main;
Of his dominion may no end be known,
And greater than his father's be his throne;
Beyond Love's Kingdom let him stretch his pen!"
He paus'd, and all the people cried, "Amen."
Then thus continued he: "My son, advance
Still in new impudence, new ignorance.
Success let others teach, learn thou from me
Pangs without birth, and fruitless industry.
Let Virtuosos in five years be writ;
Yet not one thought accuse thy toil of wit.
Let gentle George in triumph tread the stage,
Make Dorimant betray, and Loveit rage;
Let Cully, Cockwood, Fopling, charm the pit,
And in their folly shew the writer's wit.
Yet still thy fools shall stand in thy defense,
And justify their author's want of sense.
Let 'em be all by thy own model made
Of dulness, and desire no foreign aid;
That they to future ages may be known,
Not copies drawn, but issue of thy own.
Nay, let thy men of wit too be the same,
All full of thee, and differing but in name.

But let no alien S—dl—y interpose,
To lard with wit thy hungry Epsom prose.
And when false flowers of rhetoric thou wouldst cull,
Trust nature, do not labor to be dull;
But write thy best, and top; and, in each line,
Sir Formal's oratory will be thine:
Sir Formal, tho' unsought, attends thy quill,
And does thy northern dedications fill.
Nor let false friends seduce thy mind to fame,
By arrogating Jonson's hostile name.
Let father Flecknoe fire thy mind with praise,
And uncle Ogleby thy envy raise.
Thou art my blood, where Jonson has no part:
What share have we in nature, or in art?
Where did his wit on learning fix a brand,
And rail at arts he did not understand?
Where made he love in Prince Nicander's vein,
Or swept the dust in Psyche's humble strain?
Where sold he bargains, 'whip-stitch, kiss my arse,'
Promis'd a play and dwindled to a farce?
When did his Muse from Fletcher scenes purloin,
As thou whole Eth'rege dost transfuse to thine?
But so transfus'd, as oil on water's flow,
His always floats above, thine sinks below.
This is thy province, this thy wondrous way,
New humors to invent for each new play:
This is that boasted bias of thy mind,
By which one way, to dulness, 't is inclin'd;
Which makes thy writings lean on one side still,
And, in all changes, that way bends thy will.
Nor let thy mountain-belly make pretense
Of likeness; thine 's a tympany of sense.
A tun of man in thy large bulk is writ,
But sure thou 'rt but a kilderkin of wit.
Like mine, thy gentle numbers feebly creep;
Thy tragic Muse gives smiles, thy comic sleep.
With whate'er gall thou sett'st thyself to write,
Thy inoffensive satires never bite.
In thy felonious heart tho' venom lies,
It does but touch thy Irish pen, and dies.
Thy genius calls thee not to purchase fame
In keen iambics, but mild anagram.
Leave writing plays, and choose for thy command

Some peaceful province in acrostic land.
There thou may'st wings display and altars raise,
And torture one poor word ten thousand ways.
Or, if thou wouldst thy diff'rent talents suit,
Set thy own songs, and sing them to thy lute."
    He said: but his last words were scarcely heard;
For Bruce and Longvil had a trap prepar'd,
And down they sent the yet declaiming bard.
Sinking he left his drugget robe behind,
Borne upwards by a subterranean wind.
The mantle fell to the young prophet's part,
With double portion of his father's art.

TO THE MEMORY OF MR. OLDHAM

[John Oldham, after Dryden and Butler the ablest satirist of the
Restoration period, died on December 9, 1683, at the age of thirty.
To an edition of his *Remains in Verse and Prose,* published late in
the next year, Dryden prefixed the following noble tribute.]

Farewell, too little, and too lately known,
Whom I began to think and call my own:
For sure our souls were near allied, and thine
Cast in the same poetic mold with mine.
One common note on either lyre did strike,
And knaves and fools we both abhorr'd alike.
To the same goal did both our studies drive;
The last set out the soonest did arrive.
Thus Nisus fell upon the slippery place,
While his young friend perform'd and won the race.
O early ripe! to thy abundant store
What could advancing age have added more?
It might (what nature never gives the young)
Have taught the numbers of thy native tongue.
But satire needs not those, and wit will shine
Thro' the harsh cadence of a rugged line:
A noble error, and but seldom made,
When poets are by too much force betray'd.
Thy generous fruits, tho' gather'd ere their prime,
Still shew'd a quickness; and maturing time
But mellows what we write to the dull sweets of rhyme.

Once more, hail and farewell; farewell, thou young,
But ah too short, Marcellus of our tongue;
Thy brows with ivy, and with laurels bound;
But fate and gloomy night encompass thee around.

A SONG FOR ST. CECILIA'S DAY, 1687

[About 1683 a musical society in London began the custom of celebrating November 22, the Feast of St. Cecilia, the patroness of music, by a public concert. Dryden wrote the following ode, which was set to music by an Italian composer, Giovanni Battista Draghi, for the performance of 1687. So far as is known, this ode was first printed in *Examen Poeticum*, 1693. It seems possible, however, that it was published earlier, as a broadside, like its greater successor, *Alexander's Feast*. (see p. 86)]

I

From harmony, from heav'nly harmony
    This universal frame began:
    When Nature underneath a heap
        Of jarring atoms lay,
    And could not heave her head,
The tuneful voice was heard from high:
    "Arise, ye more than dead."
Then cold, and hot, and moist, and dry,
In order to their stations leap,
        And Music's pow'r obey.
From harmony, from heav'nly harmony
    This universal frame began:
    From harmony to harmony
Thro' all the compass of the notes it ran,
The diapason closing full in Man.

II

What passion cannot Music raise and quell!
    When Jubal struck the corded shell,
    His list'ning brethren stood around,
    And, wond'ring, on their faces fell
    To worship that celestial sound.
Less than a god they thought there could not dwell
        Within the hollow of that shell

That spoke so sweetly and so well.
What passion cannot Music raise and quell!

III

The Trumpet's loud clangor
    Excites us to arms,
With shrill notes of anger,
    And mortal alarms.
The double double double beat
    Of the thund'ring Drum
Cries: "Hark! the foes come;
Charge, charge, 't is too late to retreat."

IV

The soft complaining Flute
In dying notes discovers
The woes of hopeless lovers,
Whose dirge is whisper'd by the warbling Lute.

V

Sharp Violins proclaim
Their jealous pangs, and desperation,
Fury, frantic indignation,
Depth of pains, and height of passion,
    For the fair, disdainful dame.

VI

But O! what art can teach,
    What human voice can reach,
The sacred Organ's praise?
    Notes inspiring holy love,
Notes that wing their heav'nly ways
    To mend the choirs above.

VII

Orpheus could lead the savage race;
And trees unrooted left their place,
    Sequacious of the lyre;
But bright Cecilia rais'd the wonder high'r:
When to her Organ vocal breath was giv'n,

An angel heard, and straight appear'd,
   Mistaking earth for heav'n.

GRAND CHORUS

As from the pow'r of sacred lays
   The spheres began to move,
And sung the great Creator's praise
   To all the blest above;
So, when the last and dreadful hour
This crumbling pageant shall devour,
The Trumpet shall be heard on high,
The dead shall live, the living die,
And Music shall untune the sky.

EPIGRAM ON MILTON

[This epigram is engraved, without the name of the author, beneath
the portrait of Milton which forms the frontispiece to Tonson's folio
edition of *Paradise Lost*, 1688. Dryden's name is first joined to it in
the second edition, 1716, of the *Sixth Part of Miscellany Poems*.]

Three poets, in three distant ages born,
Greece, Italy, and England did adorn.
The first in loftiness of thought surpass'd,
The next in majesty, in both the last:
The force of Nature could no farther go;
To make a third, she join'd the former two.

ALEXANDER'S FEAST

OR, THE POWER OF MUSIC; AN ODE IN HONOR OF ST. CECILIA'S DAY

[Dryden wrote this greatest of his lyric poems for the celebration of the Feast of St. Cecilia (November 22), 1697. . . . It was first set to music by Jeremiah Clarke; next, in 1711, by Thomas Clayton; finally, in 1736, by Handel. . . . It was published as a folio pamphlet in 1697, and was reprinted in the volume of *Fables*, 1700. In a letter to Tonson, written about the close of 1697, Dryden says: "I am glad to heare from all hands, that my Ode is esteem'd the best of all my poetry, by all the town: I thought so my self when I writ it; but being old, I mistrusted my own judgment. I hope it has done you service, and will do more."]

I

'T was at the royal feast, for Persia won
                By Philip's warlike son:
            Aloft in awful state
            The godlike hero sate
                On his imperial throne:
        His valiant peers were plac'd around;
    Their brows with roses and with myrtles bound:
            (So should desert in arms be crown'd.)
        The lovely Thais, by his side,
        Sate like a blooming Eastern bride
    In flow'r of youth and beauty's pride.
            Happy, happy, happy pair!
            None but the brave,
            None but the brave,
            None but the brave deserves the fair.

CHORUS

Happy, happy, happy pair!
None but the brave,
None but the brave,
None but the brave deserves the fair.

II

Timotheus, plac'd on high
    Amid the tuneful choir,
        With flying fingers touch'd the lyre:

The trembling notes ascend the sky,
      And heav'nly joys inspire.
The song began from Jove,
Who left his blissful seats above,
(Such is the pow'r of mighty love.)
A dragon's fiery form belied the god:
Sublime on radiant spires he rode,
    When he to fair Olympia press'd;
    And while he sought her snowy breast:
Then, round her slender waist he curl'd,
And stamp'd an image of himself, a sov'reign of the world.
The list'ning crowd admire the lofty sound;
"A present deity," they shout around;
"A present deity," the vaulted roofs rebound:
      With ravish'd ears
      The monarch hears,
      Assumes the god,
      Affects to nod,
And seems to shake the spheres.

CHORUS

With ravish'd ears
The monarch hears,
Assumes the god,
Affects to nod,
And seems to shake the spheres.

III

The praise of Bacchus then the sweet musician sung,
  Of Bacchus ever fair and ever young:
    The jolly god in triumph comes;
    Sound the trumpets; beat the drums;
      Flush'd with a purple grace
      He shews his honest face:
Now give the hautboys breath; he comes, he comes.
    Bacchus, ever fair and young,
      Drinking joys did first ordain;
    Bacchus' blessings are a treasure,
    Drinking is the soldier's pleasure:
      Rich the treasure,
      Sweet the pleasure,
      Sweet is pleasure after pain.

CHORUS

Bacchus' blessings are a treasure,
Drinking is the soldier's pleasure:
  Rich the treasure,
  Sweet the pleasure,
 Sweet is pleasure after pain.

IV

 Sooth'd with the sound, the king grew vain;
  Fought all his battles o'er again;
And thrice he routed all his foes; and thrice he slew the slain.
The master saw the madness rise;
His glowing cheeks, his ardent eyes;
And, while he heav'n and earth defied,
Chang'd his hand, and check'd his pride.
  He chose a mournful Muse,
   Soft pity to infuse:
He sung Darius great and good,
  By too severe a fate,
Fallen, fallen, fallen, fallen,
  Fallen from his high estate,
   And welt'ring in his blood;
Deserted, at his utmost need,
By those his former bounty fed;
On the bare earth expos'd he lies,
With not a friend to close his eyes.

With downcast looks the joyless victor sate,
 Revolving in his alter'd soul
  The various turns of chance below;
 And, now and then, a sigh he stole;
  And tears began to flow.

CHORUS

Revolving in his alter'd soul
 The various turns of chance below;
And, now and then, a sigh he stole;
 And tears began to flow.

V

The mighty master smil'd, to see
That love was in the next degree:
'T was but a kindred sound to move,
For pity melts the mind to love.
   Softly sweet, in Lydian measures,
   Soon he sooth'd his soul to pleasures.
"War," he sung, "is toil and trouble;
Honor, but an empty bubble;
   Never ending, still beginning,
Fighting still, and still destroying:
   If the world be worth thy winning,
Think, O think it worth enjoying;
   Lovely Thais sits beside thee,
   Take the good the gods provide thee."

The many rend the skies with loud applause;
So Love was crown'd, but Music won the cause.
   The prince, unable to conceal his pain,
     Gaz'd on the fair
     Who caus'd his care,
   And sigh'd and look'd, sigh'd and look'd,
  Sigh'd and look'd, and sigh'd again:
At length, with love and wine at once oppress'd,
The vanquish'd victor sunk upon her breast.

CHORUS

The prince, unable to conceal his pain,
     Gaz'd on the fair
     Who caus'd his care,
   And sigh'd and look'd, sigh'd and look'd,
  Sigh'd and look'd, and sigh'd again:
At length, with love and wine at once oppress'd,
The vanquish'd victor sunk upon her breast.

VI

Now strike the golden lyre again:
A louder yet, and yet a louder strain.

Break his bands of sleep asunder,
And rouse him, like a rattling peal of thunder.
  Hark, hark, the horrid sound
   Has rais'd up his head:
   As awak'd from the dead,
  And amaz'd, he stares around.
"Revenge, revenge!" Timotheus cries,
  "See the Furies arise!
  See the snakes that they rear,
  How they hiss in their hair,
 And the sparkles that flash from their eyes!
  Behold a ghastly band,
  Each a torch in his hand!
Those are Grecian ghosts, that in battle were slain,
   And unburied remain
   Inglorious on the plain:
   Give the vengeance due
   To the valiant crew.
Behold how they toss their torches on high,
   How they point to the Persian abodes,
And glitt'ring temples of their hostile gods!"
The princes applaud, with a furious joy;
And the king seiz'd a flambeau with zeal to destroy;
   Thais led the way,
   To light him to his prey,
And, like another Helen, fir'd another Troy.

CHORUS

And the king seiz'd a flambeau with zeal to destroy;
   Thais led the way,
   To light him to his prey,
And, like another Helen, fir'd another Troy.

VII

   Thus, long ago,
  Ere heaving bellows learn'd to blow,
   While organs yet were mute;
  Timotheus, to his breathing flute,
   And sounding lyre,
Could swell the soul to rage, or kindle soft desire.
  At last, divine Cecilia came,
  Inventress of the vocal frame;

The sweet enthusiast, from her sacred store,
    Enlarg'd the former narrow bounds,
    And added length to solemn sounds,
With nature's mother wit, and arts unknown before.
   Let old Timotheus yield the prize,
    Or both divide the crown;
   He rais'd a mortal to the skies;
    She drew an angel down.

GRAND CHORUS

At last, divine Cecilia came,
   Inventress of the vocal frame;
The sweet enthusiast, from her sacred store,
    Enlarg'd the former narrow bounds,
    And added length to solemn sounds,
With nature's mother wit, and arts unknown before.
   Let old Timotheus yield the prize,
    Or both divide the crown;
   He rais'd a mortal to the skies;
    She drew an angel down.

Alphabetical Index of Titles and First Lines

DOVER · THRIFT · EDITIONS

All books complete and unabridged. All 5¾₁₆" x 8¼," paperbound.

A selection of the more than 200 titles in the series.

POETRY

101 GREAT AMERICAN POEMS, The American Poetry & Literacy Project (ed.). (Available in U.S. only.) 40158-8

ENGLISH ROMANTIC POETRY: An Anthology, Stanley Appelbaum (ed.). 256pp. 29282-7

DOVER BEACH AND OTHER POEMS, Matthew Arnold. 112pp. 28037-3

SELECTED POEMS FROM "FLOWERS OF EVIL," Charles Baudelaire. 64pp. 28450-6

BHAGAVADGITA, Bhagavadgita. 112pp. 27782-8

THE BOOK OF PSALMS, King James Bible. 128pp. 27541-8

IMAGIST POETRY: AN ANTHOLOGY, Bob Blaisdell (ed.). 176pp. (Available in U.S. only.) 40875-2

BLAKE'S SELECTED POEMS, William Blake. 96pp. 28517-0

SONGS OF INNOCENCE AND SONGS OF EXPERIENCE, William Blake. 64pp. 27051-3

THE CLASSIC TRADITION OF HAIKU: An Anthology, Faubion Bowers (ed.). 96pp. 29274-6

BEST POEMS OF THE BRONTË SISTERS (ed. by Candace Ward), Emily, Anne, and Charlotte Brontë. 64pp. 29529-X

SONNETS FROM THE PORTUGUESE AND OTHER POEMS, Elizabeth Barrett Browning. 64pp. 27052-1

MY LAST DUCHESS AND OTHER POEMS, Robert Browning. 128pp. 27783-6

POEMS AND SONGS, Robert Burns. 96pp. 26863-2

SELECTED POEMS, George Gordon, Lord Byron. 112pp. 27784-4

SELECTED CANTERBURY TALES, Geoffrey Chaucer. 144pp. 28241-4

THE RIME OF THE ANCIENT MARINER AND OTHER POEMS, Samuel Taylor Coleridge. 80pp. 27266-4

WAR IS KIND AND OTHER POEMS, Stephen Crane. 64pp. 40424-2

THE CAVALIER POETS: An Anthology, Thomas Crofts (ed.). 80pp. 28766-1

SELECTED POEMS, Emily Dickinson. 64pp. 26466-1

SELECTED POEMS, John Donne. 96pp. 27788-7

SELECTED POEMS, Paul Laurence Dunbar. 80pp. 29980-5

"THE WASTE LAND" AND OTHER POEMS, T. S. Eliot. 64pp. (Available in U.S. only.) 40061-1

THE CONCORD HYMN AND OTHER POEMS, Ralph Waldo Emerson. 64pp. 29059-X

THE RUBÁIYÁT OF OMAR KHAYYÁM: FIRST AND FIFTH EDITIONS, Edward FitzGerald. 64pp. 26467-X

A BOY'S WILL AND NORTH OF BOSTON, Robert Frost. 112pp. (Available in U.S. only.) 26866-7

THE ROAD NOT TAKEN AND OTHER POEMS, Robert Frost. 64pp. (Available in U.S. only.) 27550-7

HARDY'S SELECTED POEMS, Thomas Hardy. 80pp. 28753-X

"GOD'S GRANDEUR" AND OTHER POEMS, Gerard Manley Hopkins. 80pp. 28729-7

A SHROPSHIRE LAD, A. E. Housman. 64pp. 26468-8

LYRIC POEMS, John Keats. 80pp. 26871-3

DOVER · THRIFT · EDITIONS

POETRY

GUNGA DIN AND OTHER FAVORITE POEMS, Rudyard Kipling. 80pp. 26471-8

SNAKE AND OTHER POEMS, D. H. Lawrence. 64pp. 40647-4

THE CONGO AND OTHER POEMS, Vachel Lindsay. 96pp. 27272-9

EVANGELINE AND OTHER POEMS, Henry Wadsworth Longfellow. 64pp. 28255-4

FAVORITE POEMS, Henry Wadsworth Longfellow. 96pp. 27273-7

"TO HIS COY MISTRESS" AND OTHER POEMS, Andrew Marvell. 64pp. 29544-3

SPOON RIVER ANTHOLOGY, Edgar Lee Masters. 144pp. 27275-3

SELECTED POEMS, Claude McKay. 80pp. 40876-0

RENASCENCE AND OTHER POEMS, Edna St. Vincent Millay. 64pp. (Available in U.S. only.) 26873-X

SELECTED POEMS, John Milton. 128pp. 27554-X

CIVIL WAR POETRY: An Anthology, Paul Negri (ed.). 128pp. 29883-3

ENGLISH VICTORIAN POETRY: AN ANTHOLOGY, Paul Negri (ed.). 256pp. 40425-0

GREAT SONNETS, Paul Negri (ed.). 96pp. 28052-7

THE RAVEN AND OTHER FAVORITE POEMS, Edgar Allan Poe. 64pp. 26685-0

ESSAY ON MAN AND OTHER POEMS, Alexander Pope. 128pp. 28053-5

EARLY POEMS, Ezra Pound. 80pp. (Available in U.S. only.) 28745-9

GREAT POEMS BY AMERICAN WOMEN: An Anthology, Susan L. Rattiner (ed.). 224pp. (Available in U.S. only.) 40164-2

LITTLE ORPHANT ANNIE AND OTHER POEMS, James Whitcomb Riley. 80pp. 28260-0

GOBLIN MARKET AND OTHER POEMS, Christina Rossetti. 64pp. 28055-1

CHICAGO POEMS, Carl Sandburg. 80pp. 28057-8

CORNHUSKERS, Carl Sandburg. 157pp. 41409-4

THE SHOOTING OF DAN MCGREW AND OTHER POEMS, Robert Service. 96pp. (Available in U.S. only.) 27556-6

COMPLETE SONNETS, William Shakespeare. 80pp. 26686-9

SELECTED POEMS, Percy Bysshe Shelley. 128pp. 27558-2

AFRICAN-AMERICAN POETRY: An Anthology, 1773–1930, Joan R. Sherman (ed.). 96pp. 29604-0

100 BEST-LOVED POEMS, Philip Smith (ed.). 96pp. 28553-7

NATIVE AMERICAN SONGS AND POEMS: An Anthology, Brian Swann (ed.). 64pp. 29450-1

SELECTED POEMS, Alfred Lord Tennyson. 112pp. 27282-6

AENEID, Vergil (Publius Vergilius Maro). 256pp. 28749-1

CHRISTMAS CAROLS: COMPLETE VERSES, Shane Weller (ed.). 64pp. 27397-0

GREAT LOVE POEMS, Shane Weller (ed.). 128pp. 27284-2

CIVIL WAR POETRY AND PROSE, Walt Whitman. 96pp. 28507-3

SELECTED POEMS, Walt Whitman. 128pp. 26878-0

THE BALLAD OF READING GAOL AND OTHER POEMS, Oscar Wilde. 64pp. 27072-6

EARLY POEMS, William Carlos Williams. 64pp. (Available in U.S. only.) 29294-0

FAVORITE POEMS, William Wordsworth. 80pp. 27073-4

WORLD WAR ONE BRITISH POETS: Brooke, Owen, Sassoon, Rosenberg, and Others, Candace Ward (ed.). (Available in U.S. only.) 29568-0

EARLY POEMS, William Butler Yeats. 128pp. 27808-5

"EASTER, 1916" AND OTHER POEMS, William Butler Yeats. 80pp. (Available in U.S. only.) 29771-3

FICTION

FLATLAND: A ROMANCE OF MANY DIMENSIONS, Edwin A. Abbott. 96pp. 27263-X

SHORT STORIES, Louisa May Alcott. 64pp. 29063-8

WINESBURG, OHIO, Sherwood Anderson. 160pp. 28269-4

PERSUASION, Jane Austen. 224pp. 29555-9

PRIDE AND PREJUDICE, Jane Austen. 272pp. 28473-5

SENSE AND SENSIBILITY, Jane Austen. 272pp. 29049-2

LOOKING BACKWARD, Edward Bellamy. 160pp. 29038-7

BEOWULF, Beowulf (trans. by R. K. Gordon). 64pp. 27264-8

CIVIL WAR STORIES, Ambrose Bierce. 128pp. 28038-1

"THE MOONLIT ROAD" AND OTHER GHOST AND HORROR STORIES, Ambrose Bierce (John Grafton, ed.) 96pp. 40056-5

WUTHERING HEIGHTS, Emily Brontë. 256pp. 29256-8

THE THIRTY-NINE STEPS, John Buchan. 96pp. 28201-5

TARZAN OF THE APES, Edgar Rice Burroughs. 224pp. (Available in U.S. only.) 29570-2

ALICE'S ADVENTURES IN WONDERLAND, Lewis Carroll. 96pp. 27543-4

THROUGH THE LOOKING-GLASS, Lewis Carroll. 128pp. 40878-7

MY ÁNTONIA, Willa Cather. 176pp. 28240-6

O PIONEERS!, Willa Cather. 128pp. 27785-2

PAUL'S CASE AND OTHER STORIES, Willa Cather. 64pp. 29057-3

FIVE GREAT SHORT STORIES, Anton Chekhov. 96pp. 26463-7

TALES OF CONJURE AND THE COLOR LINE, Charles Waddell Chesnutt. 128pp. 40426-9

FAVORITE FATHER BROWN STORIES, G. K. Chesterton. 96pp. 27545-0

THE AWAKENING, Kate Chopin. 128pp. 27786-0

A PAIR OF SILK STOCKINGS AND OTHER STORIES, Kate Chopin. 64pp. 29264-9

HEART OF DARKNESS, Joseph Conrad. 80pp. 26464-5

LORD JIM, Joseph Conrad. 256pp. 40650-4

THE SECRET SHARER AND OTHER STORIES, Joseph Conrad. 128pp. 27546-9

THE "LITTLE REGIMENT" AND OTHER CIVIL WAR STORIES, Stephen Crane. 80pp. 29557-5

THE OPEN BOAT AND OTHER STORIES, Stephen Crane. 128pp. 27547-7

THE RED BADGE OF COURAGE, Stephen Crane. 112pp. 26465-3

MOLL FLANDERS, Daniel Defoe. 256pp. 29093-X

ROBINSON CRUSOE, Daniel Defoe. 288pp. 40427-7

A CHRISTMAS CAROL, Charles Dickens. 80pp. 26865-9

THE CRICKET ON THE HEARTH AND OTHER CHRISTMAS STORIES, Charles Dickens. 128pp. 28039-X

A TALE OF TWO CITIES, Charles Dickens. 304pp. 40651-2

THE DOUBLE, Fyodor Dostoyevsky. 128pp. 29572-9

THE GAMBLER, Fyodor Dostoyevsky. 112pp. 29081-6

NOTES FROM THE UNDERGROUND, Fyodor Dostoyevsky. 96pp. 27053-X

THE ADVENTURE OF THE DANCING MEN AND OTHER STORIES, Sir Arthur Conan Doyle. 80pp. 29558-3

THE HOUND OF THE BASKERVILLES, Arthur Conan Doyle. 128pp. 28214-7

THE LOST WORLD, Arthur Conan Doyle. 176pp. 40060-3

DOVER · THRIFT · EDITIONS

FICTION

Six Great Sherlock Holmes Stories, Sir Arthur Conan Doyle. 112pp. 27055-6
Short Stories, Theodore Dreiser. 112pp. 28215-5
Silas Marner, George Eliot. 160pp. 29246-0
This Side of Paradise, F. Scott Fitzgerald. 208pp. 28999-0
"The Diamond as Big as the Ritz" and Other Stories, F. Scott Fitzgerald. 29991-0
Madame Bovary, Gustave Flaubert. 256pp. 29257-6
The Revolt of "Mother" and Other Stories, Mary E. Wilkins Freeman. 128pp. 40428-5
A Room with a View, E. M. Forster. 176pp. (Available in U.S. only.) 28467-0
Where Angels Fear to Tread, E. M. Forster. 128pp. (Available in U.S. only.) 27791-7
The Immoralist, André Gide. 112pp. (Available in U.S. only.) 29237-1
Herland, Charlotte Perkins Gilman. 128pp. 40429-3
"The Yellow Wallpaper" and Other Stories, Charlotte Perkins Gilman. 80pp. 29857-4
The Overcoat and Other Stories, Nikolai Gogol. 112pp. 27057-2
Chelkash and Other Stories, Maxim Gorky. 64pp. 40652-0
Great Ghost Stories, John Grafton (ed.). 112pp. 27270-2
Detection by Gaslight, Douglas G. Greene (ed.). 272pp. 29928-7
The Mabinogion, Lady Charlotte E. Guest. 192pp. 29541-9
"The Fiddler of the Reels" and Other Short Stories, Thomas Hardy. 80pp. 29960-0
The Luck of Roaring Camp and Other Stories, Bret Harte. 96pp. 27271-0
The House of the Seven Gables, Nathaniel Hawthorne. 272pp. 40882-5
The Scarlet Letter, Nathaniel Hawthorne. 192pp. 28048-9
Young Goodman Brown and Other Stories, Nathaniel Hawthorne. 128pp. 27060-2
The Gift of the Magi and Other Short Stories, O. Henry. 96pp. 27061-0
The Nutcracker and the Golden Pot, E. T. A. Hoffmann. 128pp. 27806-9
The Beast in the Jungle and Other Stories, Henry James. 128pp. 27552-3
Daisy Miller, Henry James. 64pp. 28773-4
The Turn of the Screw, Henry James. 96pp. 26684-2
Washington Square, Henry James. 176pp. 40431-5
The Country of the Pointed Firs, Sarah Orne Jewett. 96pp. 28196-5
The Autobiography of an Ex-Colored Man, James Weldon Johnson. 112pp. 28512-X
Dubliners, James Joyce. 160pp. 26870-5
A Portrait of the Artist as a Young Man, James Joyce. 192pp. 28050-0
The Metamorphosis and Other Stories, Franz Kafka. 96pp. 29030-1
The Man Who Would Be King and Other Stories, Rudyard Kipling. 128pp. 28051-9
You Know Me Al, Ring Lardner. 128pp. 28513-8
Selected Short Stories, D. H. Lawrence. 128pp. 27794-1
Green Tea and Other Ghost Stories, J. Sheridan LeFanu. 96pp. 27795-X
The Call of the Wild, Jack London. 64pp. 26472-6
Five Great Short Stories, Jack London. 96pp. 27063-7
The Sea-Wolf, Jack London. iv+244pp. 41108-7
White Fang, Jack London. 160pp. 26968-X
Death in Venice, Thomas Mann. 96pp. (Available in U.S. only.) 28714-9
In a German Pension: 13 Stories, Katherine Mansfield. 112pp. 28719-X

DOVER·THRIFT·EDITIONS

FICTION

THE NECKLACE AND OTHER SHORT STORIES, Guy de Maupassant. 128pp. 27064-5
BARTLEBY AND BENITO CERENO, Herman Melville. 112pp. 26473-4
THE OIL JAR AND OTHER STORIES, Luigi Pirandello. 96pp. 28459-X
THE GOLD-BUG AND OTHER TALES, Edgar Allan Poe. 128pp. 26875-6
TALES OF TERROR AND DETECTION, Edgar Allan Poe. 96pp. 28744-0
THE QUEEN OF SPADES AND OTHER STORIES, Alexander Pushkin. 128pp. 28054-3
THE STORY OF AN AFRICAN FARM, Olive Schreiner. 256pp. 40165-0
FRANKENSTEIN, Mary Shelley. 176pp. 28211-2
THREE LIVES, Gertrude Stein. 176pp. (Available in U.S. only.) 28059-4
THE STRANGE CASE OF DR. JEKYLL AND MR. HYDE, Robert Louis Stevenson. 64pp.
  26688-5
TREASURE ISLAND, Robert Louis Stevenson. 160pp. 27559-0
GULLIVER'S TRAVELS, Jonathan Swift. 240pp. 29273-8
THE KREUTZER SONATA AND OTHER SHORT STORIES, Leo Tolstoy. 144pp. 27805-0
THE WARDEN, Anthony Trollope. 176pp. 40076-X
FIRST LOVE AND DIARY OF A SUPERFLUOUS MAN, Ivan Turgenev. 96pp. 28775-0
FATHERS AND SONS, Ivan Turgenev. 176pp. 40073-5
ADVENTURES OF HUCKLEBERRY FINN, Mark Twain. 224pp. 28061-6
THE ADVENTURES OF TOM SAWYER, Mark Twain. 192pp. 40077-8
THE MYSTERIOUS STRANGER AND OTHER STORIES, Mark Twain. 128pp. 27069-6
HUMOROUS STORIES AND SKETCHES, Mark Twain. 80pp. 29279-7
AROUND THE WORLD IN EIGHTY DAYS, Jules Verne. 160pp. 41111-7
CANDIDE, Voltaire (François-Marie Arouet). 112pp. 26689-3
GREAT SHORT STORIES BY AMERICAN WOMEN, Candace Ward (ed.). 192pp. 28776-9
"THE COUNTRY OF THE BLIND" AND OTHER SCIENCE-FICTION STORIES, H. G. Wells. 160pp.
  (Available in U.S. only.) 29569-9
THE ISLAND OF DR. MOREAU, H. G. Wells. 112pp. (Available in U.S. only.) 29027-1
THE INVISIBLE MAN, H. G. Wells. 112pp. (Available in U.S. only.) 27071-8
THE TIME MACHINE, H. G. Wells. 80pp. (Available in U.S. only.) 28472-7
THE WAR OF THE WORLDS, H. G. Wells. 160pp. (Available in U.S. only.) 29506-0
ETHAN FROME, Edith Wharton. 96pp. 26690-7
SHORT STORIES, Edith Wharton. 128pp. 28235-X
THE AGE OF INNOCENCE, Edith Wharton. 288pp. 29803-5
THE PICTURE OF DORIAN GRAY, Oscar Wilde. 192pp. 27807-7
JACOB'S ROOM, Virginia Woolf. 144pp. (Available in U.S. only.) 40109-X
MONDAY OR TUESDAY: Eight Stories, Virginia Woolf. 64pp. (Available in U.S. only.) 29453-6

NONFICTION

POETICS, Aristotle. 64pp. 29577-X
POLITICS, Aristotle. 368pp. 41424-8
NICOMACHEAN ETHICS, Aristotle. 256pp. 40096-4
MEDITATIONS, Marcus Aurelius. 128pp. 29823-X
THE LAND OF LITTLE RAIN, Mary Austin. 96pp. 29037-9
THE DEVIL'S DICTIONARY, Ambrose Bierce. 144pp. 27542-6
THE ANALECTS, Confucius. 128pp. 28484-0
CONFESSIONS OF AN ENGLISH OPIUM EATER, Thomas De Quincey. 80pp. 28742-4
NARRATIVE OF THE LIFE OF FREDERICK DOUGLASS, Frederick Douglass. 96pp. 28499-9

DOVER · THRIFT · EDITIONS

NONFICTION

THE SOULS OF BLACK FOLK, W. E. B. Du Bois. 176pp. 28041-1
SELF-RELIANCE AND OTHER ESSAYS, Ralph Waldo Emerson. 128pp. 27790-9
THE LIFE OF OLAUDAH EQUIANO, OR GUSTAVUS VASSA, THE AFRICAN, Olaudah Equiano. 192pp. 40661-X
THE AUTOBIOGRAPHY OF BENJAMIN FRANKLIN, Benjamin Franklin. 144pp. 29073-5
TOTEM AND TABOO, Sigmund Freud. 176pp. (Available in U.S. only.) 40434-X
LOVE: A Book of Quotations, Herb Galewitz (ed.). 64pp. 40004-2
PRAGMATISM, William James. 128pp. 28270-8
THE STORY OF MY LIFE, Helen Keller. 80pp. 29249-5
TAO TE CHING, Lao Tze. 112pp. 29792-6
GREAT SPEECHES, Abraham Lincoln. 112pp. 26872-1
THE PRINCE, Niccolò Machiavelli. 80pp. 27274-5
THE SUBJECTION OF WOMEN, John Stuart Mill. 112pp. 29601-6
SELECTED ESSAYS, Michel de Montaigne. 96pp. 29109-X
UTOPIA, Sir Thomas More. 96pp. 29583-4
BEYOND GOOD AND EVIL: Prelude to a Philosophy of the Future, Friedrich Nietzsche. 176pp. 29868-X
THE BIRTH OF TRAGEDY, Friedrich Nietzsche. 96pp. 28515-4
COMMON SENSE, Thomas Paine. 64pp. 29602-4
SYMPOSIUM AND PHAEDRUS, Plato. 96pp. 27798-4
THE TRIAL AND DEATH OF SOCRATES: Four Dialogues, Plato. 128pp. 27066-1
A MODEST PROPOSAL AND OTHER SATIRICAL WORKS, Jonathan Swift. 64pp. 28759-9
CIVIL DISOBEDIENCE AND OTHER ESSAYS, Henry David Thoreau. 96pp. 27563-9
SELECTIONS FROM THE JOURNALS (Edited by Walter Harding), Henry David Thoreau. 96pp. 28760-2
WALDEN; OR, LIFE IN THE WOODS, Henry David Thoreau. 224pp. 28495-6
NARRATIVE OF SOJOURNER TRUTH, Sojourner Truth. 80pp. 29899-X
THE THEORY OF THE LEISURE CLASS, Thorstein Veblen. 256pp. 28062-4
DE PROFUNDIS, Oscar Wilde. 64pp. 29308-4
OSCAR WILDE'S WIT AND WISDOM: A Book of Quotations, Oscar Wilde. 64pp. 40146-4
UP FROM SLAVERY, Booker T. Washington. 160pp. 28738-6
A VINDICATION OF THE RIGHTS OF WOMAN, Mary Wollstonecraft. 224pp. 29036-0

PLAYS

PROMETHEUS BOUND, Aeschylus. 64pp. 28762-9
THE ORESTEIA TRILOGY: Agamemnon, The Libation-Bearers and The Furies, Aeschylus. 160pp. 29242-8
LYSISTRATA, Aristophanes. 64pp. 28225-2
WHAT EVERY WOMAN KNOWS, James Barrie. 80pp. (Available in U.S. only.) 29578-8
THE CHERRY ORCHARD, Anton Chekhov. 64pp. 26682-6
THE SEA GULL, Anton Chekhov. 64pp. 40656-3
THE THREE SISTERS, Anton Chekhov. 64pp. 27544-2
UNCLE VANYA, Anton Chekhov. 64pp. 40159-6
THE WAY OF THE WORLD, William Congreve. 80pp. 27787-9
BACCHAE, Euripides. 64pp. 29580-X
MEDEA, Euripides. 64pp. 27548-5
THE MIKADO, William Schwenck Gilbert. 64pp. 27268-0

Books by Lisa Harris

SOUTHERN CRIMES

Dangerous Passage

Fatal Exchange

Hidden Agenda

THE NIKKI BOYD FILES

Vendetta

"Filled with red herrings and heart-pounding danger, *Vendetta* will leave readers anxiously awaiting Nikki Boyd's next adventure."

—Irene Hannon, bestselling author of the Private Justice series

Praise for *Dangerous Passage*

"Readers looking for a strong female protagonist and a unique murder mystery will find much to admire in Harris's work."

—Publishers Weekly

"The combination of police procedural and a Christian love story is nicely plotted, and the characters are interesting, boding well for the future of the series."

—*Booklist*

Praise for *Fatal Exchange*

"The second book of Harris's Southern Crimes series is a thrill ride from start to finish. Full of twists and turns, this exciting story will keep readers enthralled—flawed characters and all. The romance is believable and fits well within the plot."

—*RT Book Reviews*, 4 stars

"Harris's follow up to *Dangerous Passage* is packed with plenty of nail-biting action. Add her signature complex characters, a well-developed Southern setting, and a dash of romance and you have a compelling, quick read to satisfy the most rabid romantic suspense fan."

—*Library Journal*

Praise for *Hidden Agenda*

"A nonstop chase that is constantly set on high gear, fans of Lisa Harris will revel in the constant race from one place to another. Readers will most definitely be unable to catch their breath before the fantastic ending is revealed."

—*Suspense Magazine*

"Compelling page-turner. The third book in Harris's Southern Crimes series is a fitting capper to this exciting trilogy. Complex issues and truly evil villains keep the story moving quickly. Nonstop action, as well as a culprit who is not easily spotted, ratchets up the suspense."

—*RT Book Reviews*, 4 stars